Roses

SPECIES AND VARIETIES – DESCRIPTIONS AND PHOTOGRAPHS

HANNEKE VAN DIJK – MINEKE KURPERSHOEK
INTRODUCTION BY RICHARD ROSENFELD

REBO
PRODUCTIONS

© 1995 Zuid Boekprodukties, Lisse
© 1996 Published by Rebo Productions Ltd
Text: Hanneke van Dijk, Mineke Kurpershoek
Jacket design and layout: Ton Wienbelt, The Netherlands
Photo editing: Marieke Uiterwijk, TextCase
Production: TextCase, The Netherlands
Translation: Anthea Bell for First Edition Translations Ltd, Great Britain
Typesetting: Computech for First Edition Translations Ltd, Great Britain

ISBN 1 901094 33 2

Contents

	Foreword	5
CHAPTER 1	The history of the rose	6
CHAPTER 2	New varieties of roses	12
CHAPTER 3	Caring for roses	18
CHAPTER 4	Good pruning is not difficult	27
CHAPTER 5	Pests and diseases	34
CHAPTER 6	Roses in the garden	43
CHAPTER 7	Roses and their companion plants	59
CHAPTER 8	Roses in tubs and containers	84
CHAPTER 9	Old roses and English roses	89
CHAPTER 10	Shrub roses	105
CHAPTER 11	Climbing roses	116
CHAPTER 12	Large-flowered and cluster-flowered roses	126
CHAPTER 13	Miniature roses	134
CHAPTER 14	Standard roses	137
	Useful addresses	140
	Bibliography and photo credits	141
	Index	142
	Acknowledgement	144

Foreword

A rose is a rose is a rose.

Gertrude Stein

Roses are just like people. Some are thugs, ego-maniacs, invaders, scented, gentle, and some are even quick-change artists like the wonderful *Rosa* 'Mutabilis', whose petals open rich ginger-yellow, run to crimson, and promptly fall in a week.

Gardeners are always being asked what they think about when they have got two hours of crawling-about-on-your-hand-and-knees wee-ding. Some have ding-dong, imaginary argu-ments, specially when they are in the mood and have got to be really fascistic, whipping out unwanted plants. I try describing a rose to a Martian. I mean, where do you begin? How can you get over the texture, the feel, the scent, the great aerial whoosh of a 'Madame Alfred Carriere' on those metal arches at Monet's Garden, at Giverny?

The best description I know of the intoxicating way plants realign your senses comes from Penelope Mortimer's novel *The Handyman*. Here she describes how the main charcter Rebecca …

"Through one good eye and perpetual smoke saw shapes, colours and perspectives in her wilderness and heaved, dug, planted and plot-ted until they began to emerge … Her capacity for love, so misused and wasted over the years, was [now] invested in roses. No-one who did not share this passion could know the tender-ness, almost amounting to anguish, that old roses disturbed in her wary heart. During her long life she had written volumes on the varia-tions of love, but the … damasks of Paestum, the Renaissance Albas and Bourbons from the Indian Ocean and wild briars of ancient China, the blood of Christ and the purity of Mary … silenced her. This silence was the nearest approach to the state of what other people called happiness that she had ever known … Stare upwards, as Rebecca someti-mes did, and you got vertigo, became unstable on the tilting earth."

Roses are peculiar. Some rose gardens can be a bit dodgy - a uniform level of one-colour flowers, and for the rest of the year nothing but twigs and earth. But give a rose the right setting, like an apple tree to sprint into, or a shed to smother, or a hedge to flesh out, or a rope between two pillars to rung along, and you see its amazing potential.

I remember the first time I created a rose garden. I got one of the poshest, most kosher catalogues and chose 38, everything from the rarely seen crimson-pink 'Paul Verdier' to the odd little 'Watsoniana' (which was first discovered in a New York garden in 1870), to the quirky *wichurana* which is actually a trailing evergreen, and grows wild in Formosa, and has late sum-mer, white-coloured flowers.

 But plant descriptions are one thing, real roses quite another. You only find out later on that some of the accompanying photographs had been taken under a fierce, harsh sun, washing out the colour, and that others had been over-enriched. The message, I quickly learnt, is that a rose book is a bit like a travel guide. Read it, take notes, then visit the finest rose gardens, Sissinghurst and Mottisfont Abbey, Kiftsgate Court and Hodges Barn in Gloucestershire, and see how they rate in the flesh. Smell them, look into them, and see if they're right for your gar-den. Only then will you really know.

Richard Rosenfeld, East Sussex, 1996

The history of the rose

We know that roses are extremely old from the evidence of fossil roses dating from the Oligocene epoch, at least 35 million years ago: an impressively long period.

Archeological excavations have shown that roses were important in classical antiquity. The Olive Oil Tablets of Pylos, so called because they contain important information about the oil industry of the period, mention oils used for perfume, rose oil among them. Rose oil was made from roses specially grown for the purpose.

Wreaths of roses dating from the year AD 170 have been found in the excavations of graves in Egypt. The rosebuds of which the garlands were made were still so well preserved that it was even possible to determine what species they were.

Every rose has something special about it. Double or single, they are all beautiful.

The Greeks and Romans valued rose petals highly

Roses are frequently mentioned in Greek mythology. Only girls who were still virgins might wear wreaths of roses. Much use was made of roses on festive occasions. According to a Greek legend, Aphrodite was born from the foam of the sea, and wherever flakes of that foam fell white roses grew.

Roses were important to the Romans too, and they grew a great many to satisfy the demand for rose petals. The petals were used in large quantities for stuffing rose-petal cushions, for making cosmetics, in food, in perfumes and at festivals. A famous story tells how the Emperor Heliogabalus held a great banquet when he came to power. He locked his guests in the banqueting hall, and at the height of the festivities had such an enormous quantity of rose petals let down on them that a number of people were suffocated.

The expression *sub rosa* ("under the rose" = in confidence, in secret) also derives from the Romans. When roses were painted or carved in a room or on a ceiling, everything said in that room was to be regarded as confidential. Pliny wrote about rose-growing in Roman times. *Rosa gallica* was much grown at this period.

'Great Maiden's Blush' is a very old rose, known before the 15th century, and often depicted in old paintings.

The Middle Ages and the 17th century

After the fall of the Roman Empire, the rose was temporarily relegated to oblivion. The main reason for this was the rise of Christianity, for Christians regarded the rose as a heathen symbol. In the Middle Ages, however, the flower came back into favour, and as many pictures show, it became part of the cult of the Virgin Mary. Monks at prayer used rosaries, probably so called because they were made of dried rose hips. The rose, originally portrayed only in religious paintings of this time, gradually became secularized and was seen as a symbol of love.

Much information about roses can be derived from 17th-century still-life paintings: they often depict fine vases of flowers, always including roses. These beautiful cupped double roses were Centifolias; they are also aptly called "cabbage roses" in English.

The Château de Malmaison' rose collection

Roses were much grown in gardens in the late 18th and early 19th centuries. Many different new roses were bred, the cultivars of various species. It is not generally known that Napoleon was

indirectly involved in rose-breeding, spending a great deal of money on it, even if he did not personally grow the roses. His wife, the Empress Josephine, bought a château near Paris, the Château de Malmaison, two years after her marriage to Napoleon. She was attracted to the place not only by the house but in particular by its grounds.

She turned the dilapidated building into an imperial residence, and the grounds into a pleasure garden. Nothing was too much trouble for her, and her garden became one of the most beautiful in France. She was fascinated by roses, and laid out a rosarium with what was then the largest collection of roses in the world. Besides collecting roses, she acquired other rare and exotic plants, obtaining many of them from very far afield. Botanic gardens provided her with others, and she would pass them on to growers for further cultivation. Through her enthusiasm and passion for collecting, she ensured that many previously unknown plants were grown in France.

She was also the patroness of Redouté, one of the best known of flower painters. Many of the roses depicted in his famous book *Les Roses* were painted from models that came from her gardens.

Gallica roses were already being grown in Roman times, not for their hips, as with the rose shown here, but for rose petals.

The wild ancestors of our rose   Cultivated roses are descended from roses found in the wild. The best known of these wild roses, also called botanical or species roses and often classed with shrub roses today, is the Dog rose. This rose,

8

Rosa canina, is found in the wild in Northern Europe. The Scotch rose, *Rosa pimpinellifolia*, and the sweetbriar or eglantine, *Rosa rubiginosa*, also occur in the wild in Europe. In the 14th century Gallica and Damask roses were brought back from the Middle East by the Crusaders. "Old roses" is the description we now give to the roses bred and cultivated in the past before the influence of imported China roses was felt. Old roses fall into various different groups: Gallica roses, Damask roses, Alba roses, Centifolia roses and Moss roses. Bourbon roses and remontant roses are of rather later date, and are the precursors of the modern hybrid teas. Hybrid teas are now known as large-flowered roses, in contrast to the polyantha and floribunda roses developed later and now called cluster-flowered roses. Many of the so-called old roses are still cultivated today, and there are some beautiful examples among them.

China roses brought change

The advent of the China roses brought a major change into the rose-growing world. The Chinese would not admit Europeans to the interior of their country for hundreds of years, but in the 16th and 17th centuries foreigners were allowed to trade in the seaports, although they still could not travel inside China, so that it was not until the 18th century that English travellers brought roses back from the Far East. From England they were sent to France as well.

David Austin's rosarium, with cultivars of Rosa pimpinellifolia: *left,* 'Glory of Edsel', *and right,* 'Mary Queen of Scots'.

'Silver Jubilee', a large-flowered (hybrid tea) rose. This group of roses was created by crossing old roses and tea roses.

The special characteristic of the China roses was that they had a longer flowering period than the old roses then known. Consequently, China roses were used for crossing, and breeding with them produced first remontant roses, then Bourbon and tea roses, and ultimately the hybrid tea group. Characteristics of the hybrid teas are their pointed buds, large flowers and long flowering period. Polyantha roses were probably the result of crossings with a dwarf China rose. Polyantha roses bear large clusters of small flowers, and crossing them with hybrid teas produced floribunda roses, with clusters of larger flowers. Today the terms "large-flowered" and "cluster-flowered" are preferred to "hybrid tea" and "polyantha" or "floribunda" roses respectively.

The beautiful English rose 'English Garden'.

New roses, new developments

New rose varieties are still being bred all the time. Rose-breeders cross varieties and introduce new roses, while rose-growers propagate them. Demand on the part of rose experts and the public plays an important part here: in recent years there has been a greater demand for more "natural" roses with a looser, less stiff habit of growth, and flowers in softer shades. This trend goes hand in hand with current opinion and fashions in colour, colour combinations, and garden design itself. David Austin, the English rose-breeder, foresaw the present development decades ago and has bred his own group of roses, which he calls English roses. They have the habit of growth, flower shape and fragrance of old roses, and the strength of modern roses. Garden and landscape architects have also tired of formal rose-beds, and in any case today's budgets will no longer cover the intensive maintenance of rose-beds. Accordingly, rose-breeders have developed a wide range of shrub roses, also some-times known as landscape roses. These roses are treated just like other shrubs and do not need the intensive care that must be devoted to large-flowered and cluster-flowered roses. There are many ground-cover varieties among them, helping to keep mainten-ance to a minimum. Moreover, a number of these roses are grown on their own roots, which also helps to save labour, since it means there are no unwanted suckers growing from the understock. Private gardeners too are beginning to discover shrub roses, and when they see how wide a range there is available they tend to abandon their prejudice against large rose bushes with vigorous growth.

Besides the groups already mentioned there are the climbing roses, which can be divided into repeat-flowering or continuous-flowering climbers, and summer-flowering or rambler roses. Miniature roses are also available, both for growing out of doors (dwarf shrub roses) and for use indoors as pot plants. Roses have a long history, and it is still going on. If one flower above all others can be said to be outstandingly popular, then surely it must be the rose.

The English rose 'Charles Austin', named after the father of the rose-breeder David Austin.

Rosa gallica 'Conditorum', a seldom-grown Gallica hybrid.

New varieties of roses

The continuing demand for roses is certainly one of the reasons for the constant addition of new roses to the existing range.

There is a story behind every rose. Sometimes the story can be deduced from the rose's name. For instance, 'Father Hugo's Rose' (*Rosa xanthina* var. *hugonis*) is called after Father Hugo Scallan, a missionary who sent this rose from China to Kew Gardens around 1900. Madame Caroline Testout, a fashion designer of the end of the nineteenth century, herself asked the famous rose-grower Ducher to name a rose after her. The outcome was 'Mme Caroline Testout', a rose which aroused so much interest in her customers that M. Ducher's wife may well have been jealous. His next new rose, at least, was named 'Madame Pernet-Ducher' after her. However, it was not very successful, and soon disappeared from the scene.

'Madame Caroline Testout', bred by Ducher of France and introduced in 1890.

How roses are propagated

In the wild, roses propagate themselves from seed. This generative (i.e. sexual) manner of propagation enabled them to continue in existence. When people began deliberately crossing roses, it was necessary to use vegetative (asexual) methods of propagation, for if a grower always sowed the seed of a rose obtained by crossing, its off-spring would differ widely in accordance with Mendel's law. Once a good rose was bred, however, the offspring had to be exactly like the parent, and that was achieved by vegetative propagation, for instance by taking slips. It was discovered very early that roses grow-ing on their own roots can be rather weak. However, if such roses, with weak growth but beautiful flowers, were grafted on a vigorous

understock, the result was a robust plant with good flowers. Various different methods of grafting the "scion" on the "stock" have been used. Roses which are grown on their own roots, quite obviously, are not grafted.

'Bantry Bay' grown on a pillar.

Roses and breeder's rights

There is much confusion about the terminology involved in growing and breeding roses. In addition, a date is given after the name of a new rose variety, denoting the year of its introduction. The difference between rose-growing and rose-breeding is that a grower merely propagates roses, while a breeder produces new varieties. A rose-grower cannot simply grow any rose he likes. Many varieties are subject to breeder's rights. The breeder of the rose must apply for these rights, and his rose will have to undergo tests. When breeder's rights are granted, it will be for a period of twenty-five years, and the breeder pays an annual fee for them. He can allow his rights to lapse before the end of the twenty-five years. The rose-grower who propagates roses which are subject to breeder's rights must be licensed to do so by the rose-breeder. To make matters more complicated, a rose subject to breeder's rights is often registered under a name or "appellation" other than the name it bears in rose catalogues. For instance, the registered appellation of the rose 'Lavender Dream' is 'Interlav'. The appellation will sometimes indicate the breeder, in this case the firm of Interplant.

**Rose-breeders,
the people behind
the roses**

Growing new varieties is a very time-consuming business, and it used to depend on luck until, in 1870, Henry Bennett decided to give up farming and grow roses instead. He had always bred his cattle systematically, and it amazed him that rose-breeders set about their work in such a hit-and-miss manner. Other people soon adopted Bennett's ideas. The well-known 'Mrs John Laing', of 1887, is one of his roses. 'La France' (1867), which is regarded as the first hybrid tea, was bred by Guillot (fils). The firm of Guillot is still in existence, and is now being run by the fifth generation of the rose-breeding family.

Rose-breeders often have their own specialities. For instance, the Orléans firm of Barbier et Cie specialized in climbing roses so beautiful that they are still being grown. A couple of fine examples are 'Albéric Barbier', introduced in 1900, and 'Albertine', introduced in 1921.

Growing and breeding roses obviously runs in families. The family firm Cants of Colchester has been breeding roses for more than two centuries. In the 1960s there was some rivalry between two Cant cousins, who then decided to work together instead of in competition. New roses introduced by this firm are 'Just Joey', in 1972, and 'Alpine Sunset', in 1974.

Another family firm is Poulsen of Denmark. This firm, founded in 1878, has been steadily introducing excellent rose varieties such as

*'Mrs John Laing',
bred by Henry Bennett
in 1887.*

*'Peaudouce', an
award-winning rose,
in the evening
sunlight.*

'Ingrid Bergman' in 1984 and 'Kent' in 1988. An important French firm is that of the Meilland family. In 1945 they introduced one of the most famous of all roses, 'Peace'. Not only were its timing and its name perfect, it also turned out to be an extremely robust and attractive rose. Pedro Dot was the most famous Spanish rose-breeder, and we owe him 'Nevada' (1927). He is now dead, but his work is still being carried on by his son and grandsons. Ralph Moore of the USA specializes in miniature roses. He has been working in this field for sixty-five years, and has introduced many new varieties.

David Austin has been working for forty years on the breeding of new varieties of roses with the appearance of old roses but the robust qualities of a modern rose. He calls this steadily expanding group English roses.

Elsewhere in Europe, there are several rose-breeders in the Netherlands and Belgium. The Belgian rose-breeder Louis Lens has produced, among other roses, 'Rush' in 1982, 'Tapis Volant' in 1982, 'Silver Rider' in 1991, 'Pink Magic' in 1991, 'Sylphide' in 1993 and 'Guirlande D'Amour' in 1993.

Award-winning roses There are several major awards for new roses in the United Kingdom, adjudicated by the Royal National Rose Society, which tests the new varieties in its trial grounds and may award a Gold Medal or a

'Nevada', bred by Pedro Dot of Spain and introduced in 1927.

Certificate of Merit. The RNRS also awards its President's International Trophy. In the United States, the major award is the All-American Rose Selection. Further gold medals are awarded by European trial grounds in Rome, Paris, Madrid, Geneva, etc.

Every year there is an international rose show in Westbroekpark in The Hague. The first prize in this competition is the award of the title "Golden Rose of The Hague".
To date, the following roses have won the coveted award of the "Golden Rose":

1961 'Super Star'
1962 'Colibri'
1963 'Paprika'
1964 'Wendy Cussons'
1965 'Peace'
1966 'Lili Marlene'
1967 'Queen Elizabeth'
1968 'Orange Sensation'
1969 'Fervid'
1970 'Jan Spek'
1971 'Scented Air'
1972 'Cappa Magna'

'Jan Spek', winner of the Golden Rose of The Hague award in 1970.

1973 'Scarlet Queen Elizabeth'
1974 'Esperanza'
1975 'Satchmo'
1976 'City of Belfast'
1977 'Helga'
1978 'Milrose'
1979 'Paso Doble'
1980 'Amsterdam'
1981 'Maria Mathilda'
1982 'Julischka'
1983 'Fleurette'
1984 'Directeur H.J. Bos'
1985 'Rosy Cushion'
1986 'Mountbatten'
1987 'Ingrid Bergman'
1988 'Goldmarie 1982'
1989 'Trier 2000'
1990 'Mariandel'
1991 'Amber Queen'
1992 'Romance'
1993 'Rock & Roll'
1994 'Daylight'

*'Queen Elizabeth' is
a popular, robust
cluster-flowered rose.
In the foreground,
'Ballerina'.*

*'City of Belfast', winner
of the Golden Rose
award in 1976.*

Caring for roses

If roses are well planted and properly fed thereafter, they will give you years of pleasure. Your preparation and care are very well worth the trouble.

'Corrie', a large-flowered rose for people who like orange.

The kind of soil in your garden is very important when you are planning to plant roses. Fertile garden soil with good drainage and plenty of humus is ideal. Poor, sandy soil will need plenty of improvement. Heavy clay contains an above-average amount of nutrients, but its dense structure means that a great deal of water is left standing on such soil after rain, and if there is one thing roses hate it is waterlogged soil. Species or botanical roses make fewer demands on the soil than modern intensively cultivated varieties.

A sunny, airy position

In general it may be assumed that roses like sun, at least four hours of it a day, and prefer a position where the air flows freely around them. They will be more likely to develop diseases when planted in a corner or some other sheltered place, rather than in an airy situation. Roses standing in full sun against a white, south-facing wall will find life difficult; the sun will be reflected strongly against the white wall, and during the warm summer months the rose will be liable to scorch. Paving also reflects too much heat, especially whitewashed paving stones. When a rose in a container is placed on a terrace, or in a space left vacant in a paved area, it is a good idea to surround the rose with low-growing ground-cover plants and spray it with water now and then.

When you are choosing places to plant roses against wooden fencing or other wooden partitions, or near wooden bridges, etc.,

make sure the wood has not been treated with creosote. Not only roses but other plants too will show signs of scorching when exposed to poisonous gases. Nor should you plant roses under a thatched roof or a tree from which water regularly drips; they hate a steady trickle of water from above. If you are growing climbing roses against the wall of a house, or a fence, plant them at a little distance away from the foot of the wall or fence, at least 20cm (11in) away. The soil is often dry and rich in lime directly beside a house.

‘Sweetheart’, a large-flowered rose.

Various kinds of soil

If you are gardening on light to medium-heavy clay, you can consider yourself lucky. Roses are very much at home on this type of soil. It is easy to work, fairly friable and contains plenty of nutrients. In addition the acidity level is usually very good (pH between 6 and 7). Heavy clay, on the other hand, has to be intensively worked because its structure is dense, so that rainwater stands on the surface too long and lets too little air into the ground. You can start by digging sharp sand into the topsoil to loosen the structure. It is a good idea to dig soil of this type over before the winter, and feed it with organic fertilizer. Then leave it to be broken up by frost during the winter months, and plant your roses in spring. Sandy soil has the advantage of being easy to work, and it absorbs water quickly. Its drawback, however, is that it does not retain water easily, so that nutrients will be rapidly washed away. Sandy soil therefore at least

19

'Excelsa', a summer-flowering climbing rose grown on a wooden pergola.

'Nozomi' produces a cascade of small flowers.

needs enriching with plenty of compost, about 200 to 300 litres per 10 sq m (30 sq ft). If the sandy soil is acid (with a pH value below 5) the acidity must be counteracted by spreading lime in the form of agricultural powdered lime or carbonate of magnesium lime. However, be careful not to add either of these lime products in combination with organic fertilizer. Chalky soils, such as are sometimes found in coastal areas, have a pH value of above 7, which is too high for roses, but you can still do something to improve it and enjoy a strong, healthy rose. The addition of horticultural peat will improve not only the pH value but also the structure of chalky and sandy soils. Peat also holds a fair amount of moisture, so it makes a welcome supplement. However, although peat will improve the soil structure, it contains no nutrients, or hardly any, so you will also need to give organic fertilizer every year. Peaty soil itself is naturally very acid, often with too low a pH value, and here you may need to add some lime. However, peaty soils can be very moist and may hold too much water during rain. In that case it is a good idea to seek advice before deciding to plant roses in your garden; such advice can usually be obtained from your local garden centre or nursery. It is important to specify that it is roses you want to plant, so that any suggestions about suitable fertilizers apply to roses in particular.

All kinds of soil must be friable enough for the roots to make their way through the structure easily. If there is a hard layer present it must be broken up before you plant roses. A hard layer may not always be visible; it can lie at a depth which is not easily worked over, but if water is slow to sink into your garden soil, or a part of it, it shows that such a layer is present. Try to find out what the problem is by digging. Too much water is not good for roses, and you may have to think about methods of drainage if your soil holds moisture too long.

Roots need air as well as water, and there is no room for air in soil where too much water stands for too long, and the ground-water level is high. In that case you need to work the soil where you want to plant roses very well first, double-digging the ground two spits deep, about 60cm (24in). In the double-digging process the bottom 30cm (12in) is loosened and the top 30cm (12in) turned over. While you are working over the ground like this you can dig in compost, peat or sand at the same time, depending on your type of soil.

'Monique', a large-flowered rose used by David Austin for crossing.

Good planting is important

Always dig a large hole for the rose, measuring about 40 x 40 x 30cm (16 x 16 x 12in), large enough for the roots to be placed in it vertically and then spread out in the soil. It may be necessary to dig a larger hole for shrub roses and sometimes for climbing roses too. If the roots are crammed into a space too small for them they will have

'Kathryn Morley', an English rose.

difficulty in finding their way through the soil and absorbing water, so that the rose will not get off to a good start, and is more likely to be affected by disease. When you have dug your hole, stand the rose upright in it to see if you have dug it deep enough. Make sure that the union, sometimes called "bud union", where the scion has been grafted on the understock, is just below soil level. Then hold the rose firmly with one hand and fill soil in around it with your other hand. You can use the soil you have dug out of the hole, supplemented with special rose-growing compost, or on poor soil you could use rose-growing compost alone. If you have added organic fertilizer to the soil for filling in the hole, make sure it does not actually touch the roots of the plant. Weeds and bits of twig must be kept out of the planting hole too. Break up or remove any large clods of earth. When the hole around the rose has been filled you should tread the soil in firmly. Be careful not to injure the plant or its roots in the process. When you are planting in spring in dry, open weather, it is advisable to water the plant before filling in the hole with soil, and since the soil may settle slightly, some extra soil can be added. Early spring is a good time for planting roses on wet, clay soils; on sandy soils you can also plant in autumn. Provide standard roses with a stout stake to keep them from coming loose. (Some excellent special rose stakes are available.) Put the stake in the planting hole before you fill it in with soil. If you leave the job until

Rosa mollis, *an unassuming single shrub rose.*

after filling in, you will not be able to see exactly where the roots are, and the stake may damage them as you drive it in.

The beautiful flagon-shaped hips of the shrub rose 'Bourgogne'.

Roses are greedy feeders Give roses compost or stable manure every year as winter approaches. Do not dig the manure in, or the roots of the rose may be harmed. Spread it around the plant instead. Leave the compost or manure lying around the bush; rain and frost will break the manure down, and much of it will be worked into the ground by worms, thus providing valuable humus. The end result will be good, rich garden soil with an excellent structure. However, while stable manure and compost improve soil structure, they do not provide all the necessary nutrients to stimulate roses into optimum growth and good health, so you will need to feed your roses with artificial fertilizer or rose fertilizer as well. A good supplementary fertilizer for roses should contain the elements nitrogen (N), phosphorus (P), potash (K) and magnesium (Mg). Nitrogen stimulates good growth with handsome, dark green leaves and strong new shoots, so roses should have it at the beginning of the growing season. Do not give this supplementary fertilizer at the end of summer, or it will persuade the rose to put out new shoots which will not be strong enough to survive the first frosts, so that the plant will suffer a good deal of damage. Nitrogen is best given after you have pruned your roses, at the end of March, or in early April at the latest. If necessary

The union where scion has been grafted on understock needs protection in winter.

you can give more nitrogen after the first flowering period is over, particularly on sandy soils where the nitrogen is quickly washed away. Plants need phosphorus in the form of phosphates. This element is particularly important for the development of new roots and the formation of buds, flowers and eventually seeds. However, phosphates work slowly, so they should definitely be given early in spring if the plant is to get the maximum benefit. It has been proved that roses are more susceptible to diseases if they cannot absorb sufficient potash. Patent potash contains a high concentration of the element, and the second application of fertilizer, given after the first flowering period in mid-July, should consist of it. A small handful of potash fertilizer around the rose will strengthen the bush adequately. An additional advantage of patent potash is that it also contains magnesium, another important element for roses. Yellowing leaves with green veins are a sign of magnesium deficiency. Special rose fertilizer can be bought in garden centres and from rose nurseries. As the type of soil in your garden makes a good deal of difference to the amount and nature of the fertilizers you apply, no comprehensive advice on quantities can be given here; it is best to ask an expert who has analysed a sample of your soil. In general, however, we may say that roses appreciate being fed three times a year: spread compost or stable manure around your roses early in the winter (November to December), preceded, on

'Warwick Castle', an English rose, called after the castle of the same name on the occasion of the opening of the Victorian rose garden there.

acid ground, by an application of lime. The lime can also be given in spring. Quantities will be given on the packet.

Replacing old rose bushes

If you have an old rose-bed where the roses are not flowering as freely as before, and the bushes are getting weak, it is sensible to take action and plan to replace them with new plants, perhaps of another variety. As it is possible that the roses are suffering from a build-up of disease in the soil, it is advisable to dig out the existing soil to a depth of 60cm (24in) and replace it with entirely new soil. This is hard work, but definitely worth the trouble, and if you neglect to replace the soil you may well regret it when your new roses fail to give the results you hoped for.

Of course, it may be that your soil is still perfectly adequate, but that nearby trees and bushes have grown so large over the years that the roses are not getting enough sun, and may also be suffering from rainwater dripping off the trees. In that case choose another, sunnier situation for your roses.

Protecting roses in winter

In Continental climates in particular, where the contrast between winter and summer temperatures is very marked, roses may need some protection in winter. If you know that you live in an area where winter temperatures are low and frosts very hard, it is a good idea to choose roses for their robust, strong character, whereas roses

'Souvenir de St Anne's', a Bourbon rose. A sport of 'Souvenir de la Malmaison', discovered before 1916 in Lady Ardilaum's garden at St Anne's, Dublin.

Rosa x hibernica.
Shrub roses like this,
closely related to
species roses, need
less fertilizer than
cultivars.

which are not entirely winter hardy may flourish in milder areas.
When you are buying roses, then, it is advisable to find out whether
or not they are really hardy. Getting sufficient information at this
point can prevent disappointment later. If you live in one of the
harsher climatic areas and you apply compost and manure around
your roses at the beginning of winter, it is a good idea to earth them
up too. This will be necessary only for the rather more tender
varieties, not for the species roses, which are fully hardy. The
vulnerable spot in a rose is always the union, and today more and
more roses are being grown on their own roots, which makes them
stronger. However, not every rose is suitable for growing in this way.
If you place leaves, fir branches or a quantity of peat and organic
compost over the heart of the rose bush, the union will be protected.
Standard roses are also grafted on a rootstock, although much
higher up than bush roses. The union comes where the stem begins
to branch out into the head of the standard, and it should be
protected against frost and icy winds with fir branches, straw or
rushes tied around the union itself.

'Othello', an English
rose.

Good pruning is not difficult

The main reason for pruning is to keep the plant in good shape and rejuvenate it, so that it flowers more freely and produces larger blooms. Another reason for pruning is to remove old wood and thin branches, thus keeping the rose healthy and less prone to disease.

Rosa centifolia.
Shrub roses need hardly any pruning.

All groups of roses must be pruned to remove very thin wood, dead wood, and old wood which will not produce strong shoots. Suckers which come up from the understock of a grafted rose should be pruned away as deep down as possible.

Not all roses are pruned in the same way

Each group of roses calls for a different approach to pruning, so it is important for you to know which group a rose belongs to. You will need a good, sharp pair of secateurs for pruning, preferably the two-bladed kind, since it is very important that the wound you make in pruning is as clean a cut as possible. A jagged or torn cut will let water in, and disease germs can easily become established and will spread because of the moisture present in the stem.

Keep your gardening tools in good condition and make sure they are always clean. If you rub over your secateurs with fine emery paper they will stay clean and sharp. If you grease them after every pruning session they will not rust, and most important of all, do not forget to give the hinge and spring a drop of oil now and then.

When pruning, it is important to observe the form of the rose bush and the position of the buds from which new shoots will grow. Although they are small, these buds are easily spotted. You will find them in the axils of the leaves, where the leaf stem joins the main branch. In winter, when the leaf has dropped, there will be a small scar left and you will be able to see a slight swelling. This is the dormant bud which will grow out of the main branch in spring, in whatever direction it is facing, and you need to look for outward-facing buds, since if you let all the inward-facing buds grow you will end up with a poorly shaped bush, with many crowded stems in the middle. Besides being unattractive in appearance, such a rose bush will be more prone to disease, because the wind and sun will not be able to dry the crowded branches, leaves and flowers so easily. If you leave the dormant buds facing a wall when you are pruning a climbing rose, the stems will become muddled as they grow, so make sure you prune to above outward-facing buds, and then most of the new shoots your climber makes will be growing away from the wall.

It is important not to make your cut too close to the bud, but not too far above it either. If you cut too close you may lose the new growth from a bud if the stem above it dries out or freezes. Leaving too much of the stem above the eye creates an unattractive effect, although you can remedy that later on, when the weather is milder, by cutting away the ugly extra lengths of stem. All this may seem complicated at first, but once you have got the idea it is quite simple, and these rules are worth bearing in mind. You will find further details of the way to prune the various groups of roses below.

'Stanwell Perpetual', a shrub rose of 1838, which again hardly needs to be pruned.

Pruning once-flowering old roses

Old roses that flower only once a year fall into the groups of Alba, Gallica, Centifolia, Moss and Damask roses. These roses flower in June to July on wood formed the previous year, and sometimes on older wood too, but the flowers borne on the older wood are fewer and usually smaller. It is best, therefore, to prune old stems that have finished flowering in August, either right to the ground or to just above the place where a strong new shoot has formed. If there are several side shoots, leave only the lowest one on the stem. Repeat this pruning every year. If the shrub becomes too crowded it is advisable to prune away the thinnest branches as well. If the shrub has suffered winter damage it may be necessary to remove the affected parts.

'Blanc Double de Coubert', an old shrub rose of 1892, which requires little pruning.

Pruning repeat-flowering and continuous-flowering old roses

Musk, Bourbon, remontant and single Moss roses fall into this group. They are pruned in spring, usually in March, after the worst of the frosts are over. First cut out dead, damaged and thin stems. Leave four to five (sometimes seven) healthy branches which will not be so prone to disease. Make sure that the shrub retains an open shape, which will also help to keep it healthy. The remaining branches are pruned to the same length, but the shape of the shrub is sometimes improved if a few branches are pruned slightly shorter. Choose the thinnest to be shortened. In summer, simply deadhead the faded flowers. Make sure you cut down to at least the first full leaf; a full leaf consists of at least five leaflets.

Pruning shrub roses

Most botanical, wild or species roses are classified as shrub roses, and do not need much pruning, although of course it is important to keep the bush rejuvenated, prune away old branches which are not producing many flowers, and remove thin stems which give hardly any blooms.

Once you have done that, the plant can devote all its energy to making strong shoots that will produce many flowers, and sometimes a fine show of hips as well. If you keep removing a few old branches every year it will help the bush to stay young and healthy, but it is not really essential to do so.

Pruning once-flowering climbing roses

Whether or not a climber is repeat-flowering, of course it needs a certain amount of room, or as much room as you are willing to give it. Ramblers climbing up into trees are often not pruned at all, since the whole idea is to let them climb as high as possible, so that their long branches, covered with clusters of flowers, will hang decoratively down. Pruning ramblers is not always easy, either. Over and beyond this, pruning is the same as for the once-flowering old roses except that the stems are longer. Encourage the young shoots which will rejuvenate the plant by removing old stems if necessary, cutting down to the base of a strong side shoot. Bending down new shoots and tying them more or less horizontally in place will produce plenty of new growth and more flowers over a considerable length of stem. (In fact this holds true for all roses.) Again, only dead, damaged, and thin wood should be removed from these climbers in the spring.

Pruning repeat-flowering and continuous-flowering climbing roses

Climbing roses grown against the house often start into growth early because of their sunny, sheltered situation. After a mild winter and a warm spring it is a good idea to prune early in March, rather than at the end of the month. Repeat-flowering climbing roses give their best flowers, and flower most freely, on stems formed the previous year. Branches over a year old produce fewer, smaller blooms, so you want to ensure that the plant is carrying as many one-year-old stems as possible. It is also advisable to remove old stems every spring to give extra stimulus to the new ones. This is not always possible, because the bush will not form enough new stems every year to allow for the removal of the old branches; moreover, it is desirable for new shoots to form at the base, but often old branches will make strong young shoots higher up the shrub. Shoots coming from near the ground are important in ensuring that the rose keeps an attractive appearance lower down, and produces plenty of flowers where they will give most pleasure.

Bending the lower stems horizontally will help to stimulate the growth of young shoots. They will form on the curve of the older stem because the flow of sap is slowed down there. On stems growing vertically, only the top bud will put out shoots.

'The Yeoman', an English rose, is pruned like a remontant old shrub rose.

These roses flower on wood formed the same year. After flowering only the withered blooms are pruned away, down to a full leaf, which should be outward-facing. Deadheading is particularly important after the first flush of flowers, because then the bud in the leaf axil will grow out to form a new stem bearing one or more blooms.

Rosa rugosa 'White Captain', flowers and hips.

Pruning large-flowered and cluster-flowered roses

Large-flowered and cluster-flowered roses are pruned rather harder in the spring. First of all remove dead, damaged and thin branches, leaving only a few sound, strong stems. Cut these stems back to three, four or five buds. You should end with stems about 10 to 15cm (4 to 6in) long.

If your rose has an odd shape and is planted on its own, it is particularly important to pay attention to the way the buds are facing; this does not matter quite so much in a large rose-bed containing many bushes.

Pruning miniature roses

Miniature or pot roses often have a considerable number of rather thin stems. The buds on these stems are close together, making it harder to count and select them when you are pruning.

Miniature roses are pruned to a few centimetres above the ground. Make sure you leave at least two or three buds on every stem.

These roses are pruned after the winter, somewhere around the end of March, depending on the frosts.

Victorian rose box, once used for flower shows.

Pruning standard roses   Standard roses have originated in various different groups – cluster-flowered roses, English roses, shrub roses, climbing roses, large-flowered roses and miniature roses can all be grown as standards – so their pruning should always be like the pruning of their original groups.

Most standards are pruned like shrub roses. Weeping standards are climbing roses grafted on a wild understock at a height of about 1.5m (5ft). Their old branches are removed in spring and the young shoots cut back by a third. If young shoots were allowed to grow they would be too long and the shape of the weeping standard would lose much of its beauty.

Bending the stems of a climbing rose stimulates growth.

A real lover of roses will grow them even in the greenhouse.

Pests and diseases

Botanical roses, that is, the wild species,

and many of their cultivars are much stronger than roses created by crossing

and grafted on an understock.

The hips of Rosa moschata.

In addition, not all roses are perfectly suited to certain climates, and if the soil in which they are planted is not ideal, so that the shrub has its work cut out to grow and flower, it is not surprising that it is susceptible to disease if it is damaged in any way. If you love roses but do not have much time to pamper them, then it is a good idea to choose the strongest. A rose is a beautiful plant, but you want it to look sound and healthy and produce plenty of flowers. For a start, you need the best possible growing conditions, and the rose bushes must not suffer from inadequate feeding. Once those conditions are met, you still have to see that damage from pests and disease is kept to a minimum.

Most insects cause only slight damage and will not have much effect on your roses. However, some pests can be very harmful, and you will need to take measures to prevent an attack by these insects, as well as by preventing diseases.

Mildew This disease shows as a greyish-white powdery mould on the leaves and sometimes the stems and flower buds of roses. Young shoots and flowers are particularly liable to be affected. In the case of a serious infection, the growth of the rose is inhibited and young shoots may die. For a start, you should see that the rose is not so well sheltered from the wind that air cannot circulate freely around it. Lack of sun and high humidity also encourage mildew. The

disease can overwinter on old wood and fallen leaves. Its spores will develop and spread in spring, and if nothing is done to check it your roses will slowly die.

A good spring pruning removes a major source of possible trouble. You should also clear away fallen leaves in winter and throw them out or burn them. Remove and burn the wood you prune away in spring too. There are various environmentally friendly fungicides available for spraying against mildew, based on sulphur and fatty acids. Once you discover mildew, begin treating it as soon as you can, and repeat the treatment at regular intervals. Directions for use will be found on the packaging of the fungicide.

'Red Star', a healthy large-flowered rose.

Downy mildew

Downy mildew is another unattractive powdery white mould, but it appears only on the undersides of the leaves. The upper surfaces discolour with spots of yellowish-grey to purple, which later turn darker and dry up, and then the leaf falls off. Infection is chiefly in autumn, when there is high humidity in the air and drops of moisture lie on the leaves and cool off rapidly at night. Again, it is important to remove the fallen leaves.

You can spray against downy mildew too with a fungicide containing sulphur and fatty acids.

Black spot, every rose-lover's nightmare

This is a disease specifically affecting roses and appears early in spring, particularly in damp and wet weather. The disease probably overwinters on the ground, since infection begins low down on the plant and then spreads upward. It gets its name from the black spots which appear on the leaves. After a while the leaf turns yellow and falls off. Once again, it is essential to remove the fallen leaves with scrupulous care and throw them away or burn them. Do not add leaves affected by any kind of disease to the compost heap, or you will regret it next year, since the spores of moulds spread through the air easily, and a number of the little creatures that live in our gardens can help to spread them too. Choose rose varieties as disease-resistant as possible, and by way of preventative treatment you can spray regularly with an environmentally friendly fungicide.

Rust

This disease can be identified from the presence of a large number of yellow to reddish-brown spots on the upper surface of the leaves. Rust-coloured accumulations of spores form on the undersides of the leaves and later turn black. Rust can also occur on leaf stems and young shoots. The black spores overwinter on the fallen leaf. Once again, the weather plays a considerable part in the appearance of rust and the spread of the disease. Warm weather with high humidity in the air is ideally suited to the formation of rust. Remove fallen leaves and cut out infected stems, since the spores can

Left: 'Dainty Bess'.

Right: 'Mozart', a strong, very long-flowering, ground-cover shrub rose.

overwinter on them too. Make sure that the rose is as healthy as possible, and spray regularly with a biological fungicide.

Insects Insects love roses, particularly roses that are not entirely happy with their situation. Aphids, leaf-rolling sawflies, leafhoppers, red spider mites and gall wasps can make life very unpleasant for the rose.

Aphids Aphids affect a large number of garden plants. A drought early in the summer has a great influence on the spread of these pests. When there are not many aphids about they will do little damage, but if they spread fast you must take action. Aphids take a great deal of moisture out of roses, inhibiting growth and causing malformation, and generally weakening the rose. They can transmit virus diseases in the process. They secrete a sticky substance known as "honey-dew", which remains on the plant and provides ideal conditions for the incubation of diseases. You will often see young shoots and flower buds covered by greenfly.

When the attack is a minor one and you have only a few roses in your garden, it is possible to shake the insects off the bushes or wash them away with the garden hose. Aphids are lazy insects and have difficulty climbing back up the plant. However, many generations of greenfly can be born every year, so you must be on the alert and control them if necessary. Their natural enemies

'Mermaid', a strong, single climbing rose.

include ladybirds and lacewing flies. Aphids make a tasty meal for small birds too. It is very important, therefore, that anything you apply to kill aphids does not harm these beneficial creatures. Environmentally friendly pesticides to kill greenfly are widely available. A solution of spirits, soap and water or a stinging nettle solution can also be recommended as pesticides. Planting certain herbs near roses is supposed to deter aphids too, and you can always try that method.

Leaf-rolling sawfly   The damage caused by this pest is very striking: the leaves of the shrub roll up tightly inward from the edges, in reaction to substances secreted by the female sawfly. The females also lay their eggs in the rolled leaves, and the larvae will hatch out later. More of the leaves are usually affected than the females need for their larvae to develop. The larvae appear in mid-May and are fully grown at the beginning of June. They then fall to the ground and overwinter in a cocoon at a depth of 10 to 20cm (4 to 8in) below the surface. In spring the sawflies emerge and the cycle begins again.

A rose which has been attacked by leaf-rolling sawfly does not look very attractive. Infestation often occurs in roses planted near tall trees. When you see the first rolled leaves it is advisable to remove and burn them before the grubs inside can develop into new insects.

'Mme Plantier', a rose of 1835, probably a hybrid of an Alba rose and a Noisette.

Leafhoppers Leafhopper larvae are usually found on the undersides of the leaves. They do not generally do much harm, but in large numbers they will cause the leaves to fall and action must be taken, since the larvae will develop into more insects which can spread over a wide area. It is not usually necessary to use pesticides, but in cases of serious infestation use the same environmentally friendly pesticides as for aphids, and make sure that you spray the undersides of the leaves in particular.

Red spider mite These tiny spider-like creatures make a fine web on the undersides of leaves and draw sap out of the leaf cells, causing greyish-white spots to appear on the upper surface. The leaf looks sallow and falls early. Red spider mite can be very persistent, since it may occur not just on roses but on other garden plants too. It is not easy to get rid of the tiny pests, because they shelter behind their webs, and are also fairly resistant to various pesticides. Try washing as many of them as possible off the undersides of the leaves with a garden hose, or use an environmentally friendly pesticide based on organic fatty acids.

Gall wasp This fairly harmless infestation is found chiefly on wild roses. The wasp causes a prickly, hairy growth to form on the leaves. These curious galls, sometimes quite large, hardly affect growth at all, and

The hips of 'Carminetta', a glauca hybrid.

you can disregard them. Alternatively, of course, you can prune the affected part away.

Left: 'Chapeau de Napoléon', a rose of 1827, is now known as Rosa x centifolia 'Cristata'.

Other problems Mildew, black spot, rust and insects can be a great nuisance, but eelworms and canker can actually kill roses if you do not take effective action – and even that does not always help.

Right: 'Climbing Iceberg'. Climbing roses must be given the attention they need, and should stand in a sheltered but airy place.

Eelworms This infestation causes the rose to sicken because the tiny worms attack its roots, and they can no longer absorb sufficient nutrients. Eelworms are difficult to combat. Planting African marigolds among rose bushes may help to mitigate the effects, but you must still face the fact that you may not be able to save your roses. If you want to plant new roses in the same place, the old soil must be dug out and replaced by new. It is advisable to dig further down than the previous planting holes, to a depth of at least 80cm (32in), preferably even to a depth of 1m (3ft).

Die-back and canker These infections usually occur only on neglected roses. The damage appears in spring when the rose has come into growth. You will find that the buds which have just put out new shoots suddenly dry up. The stem from which the shoots were growing "dies back" from the wound made by pruning and turns brown and dry. Whole branches can die back in this way. Remove them and watch closely to make sure that other parts of the plant are not affected. The infection often begins at a place where the branch is injured. Many roses are prone to die-back, but the summer-flowering old roses seem to be quite resistant.

Climbing roses are rather prone to die-back and canker. This can be because the wind blows their long branches against something which chafes it and makes a wound. Cut affected parts back to healthy wood and burn the diseased branches. A dirty pair of secateurs can sometimes cause infection as it cuts.

What can be done? First and foremost we should try to prevent all these troubles by ensuring that the roses are as healthy as possible, do not suffer from lack of water and nutrients, and are planted in the right place. Choose healthy, disease-resistant varieties. When you do find that your roses are suffering from pests or diseases, do not make straight for chemical pesticides and fungicides. Household remedies made from water, green soap and spirits often work very well, and so do environmentally friendly sprays based on organic fatty acids. You can also dispose of pests by simple removal, for instance by picking off the rolled leaves where the leaf-rolling sawfly grubs lurk. Environmentally friendly pesticides and fungicides do not harm the environment, have a short-term effect, and destroy only pests, not beneficial creatures.

'Picture', a large-flowered rose.

Much trouble can be avoided if you choose a strong rose in the first place. Here, 'Dortmund' is combined with the large-flowered clematis 'The President'.

Combining plants with each other properly will be helpful too, and so will ensuring that birds feel at home in your garden. Always observe good garden hygiene and remove infected material.

The problem is worse where you have a great many roses planted together. If there is one susceptible rose among them it can infect the others, and more drastic measures may have to be taken. For instance, in Kew Gardens there is a notice giving information about the rose 'La France' (1867), but no specimen of the variety itself. The notice tells you that unfortunately the rose is not grown here because it is so prone to rust that it infects its neighbours.

So choose roses as robust as possible, and use environmentally friendly pesticides and fungicides. Luckily the range of these remedies is growing all the time.

'The Friar', very fragrant, one of the first English roses.

Roses in the garden

The rose is probably the most versatile of all garden plants, and can be used in many ways, for instance in a collection of roses, in a rose-bed, climbing a tree, or against the house. There is also a great range of flower colours available. In short, no garden should be without roses.

Two things are essential in a rose garden: plenty of sun, and fertile, well-drained soil. The rest is up to you. If you love roses but live in a modern house with a garden measuring only about 5 x 10m (16 x 33ft), you need not give up any idea of having a rose garden. The most important factor is always the amount of sun your garden gets. For a start, plant as many roses as you like against walls and fences. Some climbing roses will be happy with little full sun provided they get enough light. Among them are the incomparable pale pink 'New Dawn', the red 'Parkdirektor Riggers', the beautiful fuchsia-pink 'Pink Cloud', and among the once-flowering roses there is 'Albéric Barbier', cream with a hint of yellow in the buds, and 'Félicité et Perpétue', cream with a pink shade to the buds, 'Gloire de Dijon', buff yellow with a pink blush, the pink-tinged white 'Mme Alfred Carrière', the pale pink 'Mme Grégoire Staechelin', the single yellow 'Mermaid', the wonderfully fragrant pink 'May Queen', the pale yellow 'Paul's Lemon Pillar', and the magenta to lilac 'Veilchenblau'.

Robust climbing roses can grow over a summerhouse and into a tree.

If you get plenty of sun in your garden, it is a nice idea to make a sitting area with a rose-covered pergola, or a standard rose on either side of it, or you can use metal trelliswork to support a fairly slow-growing climbing rose. You can also plant groups of roses among the perennials: shrub roses to provide the taller accents, lower-growing dwarf shrub roses near the front of the border.

A rose-bed If you are planning a real rose garden where roses predominate strongly, it is a good idea to divide it into areas that are not too large and are surrounded by low hedging. Box, *Buxus*, is often used for this purpose, not only because it makes an easily maintained hedge but also because it is evergreen. In addition, *Buxus* seems to have a beneficial effect on the growth of roses. As well as box, lavender is suitable as a hedge around rose-beds. Its grey-green foliage makes a pretty frame for the roses, and its blue flowers in summer are delightfully fragrant. However, lavender is not to be recommended quite so highly for planting around roses that are very strongly scented themselves; all that fragrance can be rather too much of a good thing. An alternative is low-growing berberis such as *Berberis buxifolia* 'Nana' and various cultivars of *Berberis thunbergii*. 'Atropurpurea Nana' and the rather smaller 'Bagatelle' have red leaves. 'Kobold' is a pretty, low-growing, green-leaved berberis. The germander, *Teucrium lucidrys*, is a shrub growing to 40cm (16in) with small, shiny green leaves and a purplish-pink flower spike borne in June to September. This shrub is generally sold as a perennial, but it too is suitable as edging around a rose-bed. If you use it of course you must be careful with your colour combinations. A rose garden of this kind is usually symmetrical and rather formal in design, so do not plant too many different roses, and make sure you preserve symmetry. Rectangular areas surrounded by a low

A beautiful rose border in Anneke van der Kraan's garden.

hedge or edging can also be used elsewhere; for instance, you could place square or rectangular beds on both sides of the path to your front door, with narrow brick paths running between them. Formal beds like these should be symmetrically planted. You could put a standard rose in the middle of each bed, or a rose pillar with a climber growing up it. Of course it depends on the space you have available whether you must confine yourself to just a few rose bushes, or whether you can fit in a standard rose or a rose pillar. Many front gardens on modern housing estates are rather small, but will easily accommodate a few neat rose-beds. You could put three similar beds side by side, or have two areas with a space in the middle of each for a pretty container planted with annuals.

You may have a fair-sized terrace directly bordering your lawn. The effect of a stretch of paving can be boring, but you could relieve it by leaving a few spaces unpaved and planting fragrant roses in them. This is a pleasing way of softening the effect, and will make the garden suddenly look much more striking.

Rose arches and pergolas

Climbing roses need support in one form or another. A rose arch is one way of providing it. You can buy metal arches suitable for all kinds of climbing plants, including roses, from garden centres and nurseries. Many gardeners like the idea of a romantic arch of this kind, overgrown and covered with clusters of beautifully fragrant

TIP

Plant low-growing shrub roses and English roses in groups of three, at a distance of 30cm (12in) from each other. They will form an attractive bushy shrub. Treat the group as a single plant for the best effect.

'Excelsa' grown as a weeping standard.

roses, perhaps with a fine clematis growing through them. However, the question is often where to find a suitable place in the garden to put this ideal into practice. An arch cannot just be set down anywhere by itself. It can be incorporated into a wooden fence or a hedge, marking the entrance or leading the eye on to an attractive view. A rose arch can also form a division between two separate areas of the garden, providing access from one to the other, for instance from an ornamental garden to a kitchen garden. Several arches arranged behind each other would make a fragrant floral avenue leading to a secluded corner with a garden seat. Or you can put several rose arches around a terrace to make a kind of arbour, creating a sheltered, private sitting area. There would be room for several climbing plants in such a design, so you could plant not only a few repeat-flowering climbers, but also some plants which may flower less continuously but are worth growing for their magnificent blooms. They could be roses which flower less freely than the continuous-flowering varieties, or clematis and wisteria, either purple wisteria or a white cultivar. Honeysuckle can also be combined with roses, but remember that it is highly scented, and if you happen to have a keen sense of smell its fragrance could clash with the scent of the roses.

Make sure there is always a different plant in bloom, and you will be able to enjoy various flower shapes and colours over a long period.

A romantic rose arch in the Rhulenhof, with Rosa 'Zéphirine Drouhin' growing over it.

'White Wings', a single, large-flowered rose. This rose calls for a certain amount of care.

On the other hand, don't overdo it, or much of the effect of the individual flowers will be lost.

In most cases a wooden trellis can be used instead of a metal rose arch. Garden centres and DIY stores sell various useful packs of timber from which you can build your trelliswork.

A rose in a tree

For some reason roses are planted to clamber up trees more often in Great Britain than on the Continent of Europe. In the United Kingdom, robust summer-flowering climbing roses, properly known as ramblers, are often planted against trees and sheds or other outbuildings.

In general, roses with this very strong habit of growth are species roses or their cultivars. They use their long and very thorny branches to haul themselves into a tree and then climb up it, or even cover whole sheds. In their flowering season they are profusely laden with innumerable trusses of flowers, and at this time, as if by magic, your shed or tree becomes a vast bouquet. There is a famous arbour at Sissinghurst Castle covered by *Rosa longicuspis* and standing above a well at the junction of two paths. When this rose is in bloom its display resembles an enormous bouquet of white flowers, so profuse that there is hardly a leaf in sight. Once you have seen this opulent display you will want such a rose, and be happy to accept the fact that it flowers only once a year. You must be patient too, for tree-

Following page: The wonderful rose garden at Bateman's in East Sussex, England. The famous writer Rudyard Kippling once lived here.

Stout trellises give climbing roses the support they need and air around them.

Rosa 'Seagull'.

Rosa longicuspis.

climbing ramblers take several years to reach their best. A number of other summer-flowering ramblers suitable for growing into trees are the white, fragrant *Rosa filipes* and its cultivar 'Kiftsgate', 'Bobbie James', 'Seagull' and 'Rambling Rector', all of them also white, and the creamy, fragrant 'Félicité et Perpétue' and 'Wedding Day', the pale yellow 'Paul's Lemon Pillar', the pale pink 'Paul's Himalayan Musk', the pink 'Kew Rambler' and the fragrant violet-blue 'Veilchenblau'. *Rosa multiflora* is also good for climbing trees.

You will find *Rosa* 'New Dawn' mentioned several times in this book. This continuous-flowering climber is very strong and healthy, and consequently extremely popular. It is one of the few continuous-flowering roses that can also be ·planted to climb a tree. Besides the species and their cultivars named above you will find other very rampant roses available, mentioned in the descriptions of climbing roses in Chapter 12, and you can make your own choice and adorn a high wall, an old shed or an apple tree with your favourite rose.

A climbing rose on a fence

There are several climbing roses that do not grow too exuberantly and can be trained against low fences to provide some colour with their flowers. Good examples are the red 'Aloha', the white, semi-double, small-flowered 'Guirlande d'Amour', the summer-flowering, fragrant, ochre 'Buff Beauty', and another rose which flowers only

once, 'Raubritter', with beautiful cupped pink flowers. Climbing roses are not the only group that can be trained against low fences to form a delightful flowering partition; low-growing shrub roses with long, flexible branches are well suited to the same purpose. However, they must be tied in securely or they will soon be straggling everywhere. The effect will still be pretty, but not always practical or exactly what you want. 'The Fairy' is a rose suitable for such treatment. This continuous-flowering cultivar produces many clusters of small, semi-double flowers over a long period. 'Excelsa' is very similar, but with red flowers. Unfortunately 'Excelsa' flowers only once a year, but when it flowers it does so profusely. To provide an attractive look later in the season, you could grow a clematis or honeysuckle through the rose, or combine it with another, repeat-flowering rose.

Other roses suitable for growing on fences are the deep pink 'Devon', the light pink 'Essex', the warm pink 'Fair Play', the dusky pink 'New Face', the pink 'Tapis Volant', and 'Immensee', 'Snow Ballet', and 'Swany' (all three of them white), to name only a few.

A climbing rose against the house

There are a great many climbing roses suitable for growing against the wall of a house. You could plant a beautifully scented rose by your front door or French windows, preferably a continuous- or

Rose garden of Penhurst Place in England.

repeat-flowering variety. Imagine being woken in the morning by the delicate scent of roses! Here is a selection from the wide range of climbing, fragrant, continuous-flowering roses: 'Abraham Darby', apricot-coloured; 'Clair Matin', pearly pink; 'Compassion', peach; 'Coral Dawn', coral pink; 'Sympathie', velvety red; and the beautiful carmine 'Zéphirine Drouhin'.

Bear in mind that such roses will need some support, since they do not really climb of their own accord. Nails are often knocked into the wall, and the long tendrils of the rose are secured to them. The trouble with this method is that the rose is held too close to the wall, so that the wind cannot blow through it easily, and disease is more likely to attack. Moreover, the wall may get too warm in a hot summer, and then the branches and leaves will singe, particularly on a south-facing wall. It is better to provide a good framework before you plant the rose; then you can tie in the shoots wherever you want. Such a framework may consist of trellis or reinforced steel (on sale from builders' merchants), but wide-meshed plastic-covered wire netting is very satisfactory too. Get your framework made to measure and then fix it to stand a few centimetres away from the wall.

Of course other climbers as well as roses can be grown against the walls of a house, and those which climb by twining will also require some space between the wall and the framework.

The climbing rose 'Bantry Bay' combined with clematis.

Planting standard roses with care

Standard roses are grown on a rootstock, usually from a wild rose. The rose that forms the head may be a cluster-flowered rose, a large-flowered rose or an English rose, or one of the many other kinds of rose. The height of the stem can vary considerably, and it also depends on the type of rose to be grafted on it. When the rose has an upright habit of growth the stem need not be particularly tall, but if it has long, drooping branches the height of the stem will be at least 1.25m (4ft 1in). A miniature rose or dwarf shrub rose on a stem of this height would look rather silly, so because the head of such a standard is small, the height of the stem is kept to about 80cm (32in). When buying, make sure that the head of the rose is a good round shape. This shape is produced by grafting two or three scions on the stock.

It is advisable to support the stem, since when the head is in full leaf and flower it can be rather heavy. Of course you can drive an ordinary stake in beside the rose, but there are special rose stakes available too, often prettily decorated. Standard roses are best positioned among low-growing plants, on the terrace, or in grass. When you are underplanting standard roses, always make sure that the shape of the rose is well displayed. Two-thirds of the stem must always be visible. Weeping standards should definitely be placed in a very low planting scheme or they will not show to good advantage; their drooping tendrils will touch the plants underneath, and the

'Peaudouce', a large-flowered rose of 1985.

A climbing rose grown on a conservatory looks pretty from both inside and outside.

effect of the rose's shape will be spoiled. The vulnerability of standards in winter was discussed in Chapter 4 above, on pruning. Standard roses can be planted among low ground-cover plants in a neat bed with a little hedge around it, or in a bed made in the terrace, or in a lawn. Small-flowered and miniature roses grown as standards look pretty in containers, and they can be grown in that way so long as you give them fertilizer regularly (see Chapter 8 for roses as container plants). The best standards for growing in containers are roses whose stems are not too tall. The pink 'The Fairy' looks very pretty as a container-grown standard, since it is robust and has a particularly long flowering period. Other standards grown on a stem about 80cm (32in) high are the deep pink 'Devon', the pink 'Essex' and the white 'Kent'. You will find a number of other examples of roses suitable for growing as standards in Chapter 15 below. Continuous-flowering shrub roses which are suitable for growing as standards include some single roses, such as the pale pink 'Ballerina', the red 'Chimo', the lilac-pink 'Lavender Dream', the pale pink 'Nozomi' and the yellow 'Yellow Fleurette'. There is a white cultivar of this rose, 'White Fleurette', as well as the salmon-pink 'Fleurette'.

A rose arch need not be in a rosarium, but will fit into any garden.

A rose hedge Hedges usually consist of a single species of plant, such as privet, hawthorn (*Crataegus monogyna*), hedge maple (*Acer campestre*),

hornbeam (*Carpinus betulus*), beech (*Fagus sylvatica*), or various evergreen shrubs such as holly (*Ilex aquifolium*) or yew (*Taxus baccata*). If the hedge is the background to a border, it is a good idea to keep it as restful to the eye as possible, so that it sets off the flowering shrubs and perennials in front of it well. If the hedge is free-standing, for instance marking the division between a lawn and a path, or beside a grassy area, it can be a combination of different shrubs including a few species roses, or it could be a hedge consisting entirely of one of the many roses suitable for this purpose. A hedge consisting of different shrubs might have hedge maple as the major part, with additional hawthorn, hazel (*Corylus avellana*), cornel cherry (*Cornus mas*), blackthorn (*Prunus spinosa*) or various other shrubs, and such a selection (but do not make it too varied) can include roses too. *Rosa rugosa* is extremely suitable, and there are also a great many other roses, mostly species roses, which can be used for hedging. However, before deciding to plant a hedge consisting entirely of roses, you should think hard about several things.

A hedge of, say, *Rosa rugosa* is very beautiful, but like *Rosa virginiana* and its rather shorter cultivar 'Harvest Song' it makes rather a lot of root suckers, so that the hedge will become wider and wider unless you keep cutting the suckers out. *Rosa nitida* is very pretty when used for a low hedge. *Rosa rugotida* has pink flowers,

A hedge of flowering roses.

'Lavender Dream', a compact shrub rose bred in the Netherlands, suitable for ground cover. Introduced by the firm of Interplant in 1984.

Rosa 'Queen of Denmark'.

unfortunately not followed by hips. The rose grows to about 1m (3ft) high and forms a bushy shrub. It too spreads by producing many root suckers. The Scotch rose or burnet rose, *Rosa pimpinellifolia*, grows rather taller, to about 1.5m (5ft). The flowers, pale pink to cream, borne in late spring, are followed by black hips.

Rosa x *mariae-graebnerae*, a rose which is to some extent repeat-flowering, makes a very pretty hedge, with fragrant, silvery-pink flowers and beautifully coloured leaves in autumn. This rose too produces rather a lot of root suckers.

If you have a really large garden where you can plant a hedge that will grow, over the years, to a width of 1m (3ft) and a height of some 2m (6ft), then you might consider a number of shrub roses, such as the Dog rose, *Rosa canina*, *Rosa glauca*, with small pink single flowers which are beautifully set off by the matt, purplish-grey foliage, *Rosa moyesii* and its beautiful cultivars 'Geranium' and 'Ina Belder', which produce a good crop of fine hips after the red flowers which appear in June, and the pink-flowered *Rosa rubiginosa*. All these botanical or species roses bear hips, which means they often provide a spectacular display of colour in autumn, a very attractive sight. Birds will be grateful to you for planting a hedge of these wild roses, where they can find not only food but ideal nesting sites among the densely crowded, thorny branches. Their enemies will not find them so soon in this prickly, tangled jungle.

Ground-cover
roses

A number of roses with rather slack stems grow more or less horizontally, and so are often described as ground-cover roses. They will cover quite a large area if several are planted close together. Obviously a group of these roses is not so suitable for the small, formal garden. Such a rose can be planted alone as a dot plant among low ground cover in a small garden, but then of course the rose itself can hardly be called a ground-cover plant. Many ground-cover roses are grown in the green central reservations down the middle of major roads, and in public gardens. They provide colour on the long, narrow strips between motorway lanes, bicycle lanes and footpaths, and are useful in large groups in public parks. The Darthuizen nurseries of Interplant, and the French rose-breeding firm of Meilland, have specialized in growing roses with a rather low, spreading habit of growth, suitable for planting on slopes and covering large areas.

There are both summer-flowering and continuous-flowering roses in this group. The continuous-flowering varieties are naturally the most attractive for the private garden, since it seems wasteful to devote an area of several square metres to a plant that flowers only once a year. Summer-flowering ground-cover roses are to be recommended only if you have a pronounced slope that can do with some variation in its planting. Examples of such roses are the white field rose, *Rosa arvensis*, *Rosa paulii*, also white, and the pink 'Max

Rosa *'Aurora'*.

Graf', a hybrid of *R. rugosa*. There is also a white-flowering cultivar of this rose, 'White Max Graf', and a red cultivar, 'Red Max Graf'. *Rosa* 'Pink Spray' and *Rosa* 'White Spray' are respectively pink- and white-flowering. During the main flowering season these shrubs disappear under their burden of many little flowers borne close together in conical clusters. Occasional new flower trusses form after the main, lavish flowering. The foliage of these roses remains on the plant for quite a long time, and in a fairly mild winter may even stay on the shrub until early spring. The white cultivar grows a little more robustly than the pink cultivar.

Good continuous-flowering ground-cover roses which do not spread too exuberantly, and are therefore suitable for normal garden planting schemes, include the blood-red 'Eyeopener' (height 40cm [16in], planting distance 50cm [20in]), the white 'Swany' (40–60cm [16–24in] in height, planting distance 50cm [20in]), and 'Devon' (height 50cm [20in], planting distance 60cm [24in]).

Roses which spread rather more widely are the pale pink 'Essex', the white 'Kent', the single pink to white 'Nozomi' and the pink 'The Fairy'. Ground-cover roses which grow to a width of at least 1m (3ft) are suitable only for large beds. Others worth mentioning, besides the cultivars named above, are 'Ferdy', pink, and 'Tapis Volant', pink and white.

'Little White Pet', a dwarf shrub rose suitable for ground cover.

Ground-cover roses such as 'Kent' can also be grown as standards.

Roses and their companion plants

Roses combine extremely well with other plants, for instance shrubs, perennials and annuals. The choice of combinations is almost unlimited.

In recent years the way roses are planted in the garden has changed a great deal. Whereas a few years ago they were still planted uncompromisingly in a formal bed with nothing but black soil around them, they now tend to be grown among other plants in the herbaceous border, or among shrubs in a shrub border. Where roses are still grown in rose-beds we now prefer to plant perennials or annuals between them, so that the soil is hidden.

The choice of garden plants, like the interior decoration of a house, is a very individual matter. Some people like soft colours and shades that are close to each other in the spectrum, others prefer strong, perhaps contrasting colours. You will find a few suggestions below for combining roses with perennials and annuals.

Pink and red roses combine well with blue flowers.

White roses   White, of course, will combine easily with any other colour; it never clashes. White roses can be grown among other white-flowered plants, perhaps with the addition of grey-leaved foliage plants. Pale blue, pink, or lemon-yellow flowers can be added to the combination of white with grey-leaved plants.

White roses also make pretty accents in a yellow and green border, or a border of predominantly pink, blue, and lilac shades, with grey-leaved plants which once again provide the eye with an attractive transition.

TIP
A rose should never be hidden among other plants, or it will get too wet in damp weather and diseases may easily attack it. So choose much lower or very sparse underplanting close to roses.

*'White Captain',
a Rugosa hybrid.*

Yellow roses Just as white roses create light accents in a yellow border, yellow roses can serve the same purpose in a predominantly white planting scheme. Cream and pale yellow roses are best for creating this effect. since they are not too much of a contrast with all the white, but merely enliven the planting. A deeper yellow rose will combine well with green and yellowish-green shades, and another possibility is to grow one with pale to deep blue flowers, or for a warmer effect with flowers of pale to deep orange.

Apricot and peach-coloured roses Very pale orange, apricot or peach-coloured roses are often so subtly tinted that it is a pity to let them be submerged in a multi-coloured planting scheme. Roses of these colours are best grown combined with other pale shades. Yellowish-green and pale blue-flowering plants make good companions. If the colour of the rose has a touch of pink in it, you could add pink or mauve plants. If it is more of an orange shade, it could be combined with pale yellow or muted orange flowers.

Orange to orange-red roses Bright orange to orange-red is often so emphatic a colour that there is no fear of its failing to attract attention. A combination with various shades of blue and some additional notes of yellowish-green is particularly attractive. Yellow or orange can be chosen instead of blue.

Scarlet to crimson roses

You need to be a little careful with red roses. It can be difficult to combine them with other shades of red and pink, more difficult than combining them with yellow or blue flowers. Red may incline towards either orange or purple, and if these two different shades of red grow next to each other they can clash and make an unattractive effect.

Consequently, roses that lean towards orange in colour will look best with yellowish-green, yellow and orange flowers, perhaps with the addition of a few pretty blue-flowering plants. Roses with a touch of purple or lilac are better combined with blue, pink and purple flowers. We have seen a border containing a number of lemon-yellow, yellow, bronze and orange flowers with a single red rose, and the bright, sunny effect was very pleasing.

Following page: 'Sir Walter Raleigh', an English rose with flowers resembling a tree peony.

Purple roses

Bluish-purple or violet is a colour seldom found in roses; the colour is usually more of a reddish-purple. However, a few beautiful purple roses have been bred in recent years. Purple is attractive in combination with pink, blue or yellowish-green shades.

Pink roses

Pink roses come in a very wide range of shades, from soft, pale pink to shell pink or candy pink, and on to deep fuchsia pink or carmine. As with red shades, when you are choosing companion plants it is a good idea to consider whether the pink has a hint of blue or a touch of salmon in it.

'William Shakespeare', an English rose.

Pale pink roses look pretty in a white and pale pink border, or else combined with blue, pink and purple, with the addition of grey-leaved plants if you like.

Deeper shades of pink also look attractive in such a border, or in a border of mixed roses, or among pale blue flowers, with the addition of yellowish-green flowers and of attractive foliage plants such as hostas and ferns.

Roses combined with other plants make a natural effect.

Grey-leaved plants as companions for pink and white roses

Attractive grey-leaved plants include lamb's ears (*Stachys byzantina*), and the white-flowered *Anaphalis triplinervis*, which also has a pale yellow cultivar, 'Schwefellicht'. There are several pretty grey-leaved plants among the artemisias, and they combine well with roses. Low-growing varieties such as *Artemisia schmidtiana* 'Nana' or *Artemisia stelleriana* (dusty miller or beach wormwood) can be planted at the front of the border. Taller varieties of artemisias are available too. These taller artemisias spread fast, so you must watch them to see that they do not gradually choke the rose. Snow-in-summer (*Cerastium biebersteinii*) has pale silvery-grey foliage and is a creeping, mat-forming plant with white flowers.

The pink, *Dianthus plumaris*, has grass-like blue-grey leaves and delightfully fragrant flowers in many shades of red, pink and purple. There are also white-flowered pinks. *Achillea millefolium*

'Schwefelblüte' is a grey-leaved plant with pale yellow flowers. Certain grasses also have grey-green to blue-green foliage, and their structure makes a nice change in the border. A group of plants with attractive, striking foliage, such as blue-grey hostas, can also be placed in the border to provide a restful accent. Good hosta varieties are *Hosta fortunei* 'Hyacinthina', *Hosta sieboldiana* 'Elegans' and *Hosta tardiana* 'Halcyon'.

Centaurea cineraria and the pretty silver-grey *Senecio bicolor* are very attractive grey-leaved annuals.

Roses with pale to sky-blue flowers

There are a great many pale to sky-blue flowers among the perennials, including *Campanula carpatica* 'Blue Chips', *Campanula lactiflora*, *Campanula persicifolia* 'Coerulea', and the crane's-bill *Geranium sylvaticum* 'Mayflower'. Attractive pale blue varieties and cultivars are also found among the fleabanes (*Erigeron*), Michaelmas daisies and veronicas, such as *Aster novi-belgii* 'Audrey' and 'Plenty'. 'Strahlenmeer' ('Shining Sea') is a good blue erigeron.

The speedwell, *Veronica filiformis,* is a very good pale blue ground-cover plant, although people who regard this pretty plant as a weed would not agree. Decorative thistles also look attractive in a sunny rose border. The various globe thistles, *Echinops,* and the blue thistle *Eryngium,* all have pale blue to steely blue flowers and grey-

The cluster-flowered rose 'Centenaire de Lourdes' combined with lavender.

'City of Belfast', the Golden Rose of 1976.

green to blue-green foliage. Roses and delphiniums are an obvious combination. The range of delphiniums includes a number of cultivars in pale blue to deep purplish-blue, as well as some pretty pink and white varieties. Good pale blue varieties are *Delphinium* 'Clivedon Beauty', 'Gletscherwasser', 'Crown Jewel' with a black eye, and 'Loch Leven' with a white eye. Catmint, *Nepeta*, and lavender, *Lavandula*, are very good in a rose border. These plants can also be used to made an edging or low hedge around a rose-bed. Flax, *Linum perenne* (as intense a blue as you will find anywhere) and Jacob's ladder, *Polemonium*, are not grown nearly enough. *Polemonium caeruleum* grows to 70cm (28in), *Polemonium reptans* 'Blue Pearl' to about 40cm (16in), both with blue flowers. Another handsome blue-flowering plant is the scabious, *Scabiosa caucasica*. *Perovskia atriplicifolia* 'Blue Spire', a shrub with grey foliage and beautiful deep lavender-blue flowers in late summer, is very pretty and well worth growing. This plant can be badly affected by frost in a cold winter, so it is really better classified as a perennial or shrubby perennial than as a shrub.

Now that we are in the borderland area between shrubs and perennials, *Caryopteris clandonensis* and its cultivars deserve mention. These are attractive, low-growing shrubs which go very well with roses. Among the annuals, some pale to bright blue

'Blessings', a large-flowered rose.

Yellow roses combine extremely well with white-flowered plants.

examples are forget-me-nots, some of the pansies, the fluffy flowers of *Ageratum*, the daisy-like *Brachycome*, *Felicia* with its yellow centre, and *Lobelia*. *Lobelia erinus* 'Cambridge Blue' is an attractive sky-blue colour.

Blue with yellow, orange, and red roses

There are so many pure blue, violet blue and deep blue flowers that it is impossible to name them all, so we must make a selection.

Irises have not been mentioned yet, but they fit into a border with roses very well, particularly the bearded irises, the *Iris germanica* hybrids. They come in white, light blue, dark blue, purple, yellow, salmon, and deep red varieties. A group of bearded irises among ground cover of, perhaps, the alpine gypsophila *Gypsophila repens*, and next to a beautiful romantic rose, is pleasing to the eye even after flowering, because the sword-shaped iris leaves continue to provide an attractive contrast.

The range of Michaelmas daisies offers many very good varieties and cultivars in blue, mauve, and deep blue shades. There is also plenty of variety in height and flower size to choose from. Some varieties are sturdy and robust, some are more delicate and lax in their growth. An attractive Michaelmas daisy can be found for every border. Consult specialist books on the subject, or go and look in a garden centre or a nursery which carries a wide range.

Monkshood, *Aconitum carmichaelii*, is a beautiful bright blue, and

'Bantry Bay' combines very well with purple, for instance here with Clematis 'Lord Nevill'.

there are also attractive violet-blue cultivars such as *Aconitum cammarum* 'Bressingham Spire' and *A. henri* 'Spark'. The delphiniums, similar in their habit of growth, have already been mentioned among pale blue-flowering plants. The bell-flower, *Campanula*, is a rewarding plant with few requirements. There are various kinds that can be grown in a border with roses. The low-growing *Campanula carpatica* comes in shades of white or blue, and other low-growing species are *Campanula portenschlagiana* and *Campanula poscharskyana*. *Campanula lactiflora* 'Pritchard's Variety' is deep blue and grows to about 60 cm (24 in).

The herbaceous perennial and sub-shrub clematises are very striking plants, but not always easy garden plants to grow. However, they are so attractive that they cannot be omitted here. Blue-flower-ing clematises are *Clematis bonstedtii* 'Crépuscule', *Clematis durandii*, *Clematis heracelifolia* 'Côte d'Azur', and *Clematis integrifolia*. Garden geraniums, *Geranium*, come in many colours and shades. We have already mentioned a pale blue geranium, and there are also very attractive species and varieties to be found in deeper blue to lilac blue. Many geraniums have pretty leaves, so that the plant remains attractive even after flowering.

Although hyssop, *Hyssopus officinalis*, is really a herb, it can certainly claim a place in the border, and it will bring you some beautiful guests, because butterflies like to visit it. The familiar

'Dorothy Perkins', a summer-flowering climbing rose, grown with purple verbena.

'Coppelia', a cluster-flowered rose.

'Albertine' looks very attractive combined with foxgloves.

Salvia nemerosa and its cultivar 'East Friesland' could be classed with the purple-flowered plants, but there are cultivars that are more blue than purple, for instance 'Elisabeth' and 'May Night', so we will give them a place here. 'Blauhügel' is a lovely intense blue.

The herb sage, *Salvia officinalis*, has attractive grey foliage and is an excellent little sub-shrub which again is worth a place in the border. Last in the long list of blue-flowered plants, we will mention the veronicas. There are some pretty species which do not grow too tall, such as the grey-leaved *Veronica spicata* subsp. *incana* (syn. *Veronica incana*), and in particular the taller *Veronica longifolia* and *Veronica waldsteinii*, which give a rather special touch to your border planting with their strong vertical growth. There are also white and pink cultivars.

Among the annuals, some of the larkspurs have pretty blue flowers. Other annuals are the blue lace flower, *Didiscus caeruleus*; love-in-a-mist, *Nigella damascena*; petunias, of course, and some annual salvias such as *Salvia patens*, *Salvia horminum*, and the grey-leaved *Salvia farinacea* 'Blue Bedder', the last-named of which has attractive bushy growth.

'Pearl Drift', a shrub rose, combined with large-flowered clematis *and* Actinidia kolomikta.

Purple with scarlet, crimson and carmine roses

Listing blue flowers suitable as companions for roses, we mentioned some of the campanulas, and *Campanula glomerata* 'Superba' deserves mention here as well, since it is debatable whether the flowers of this plant are bluish-purple or true purple. In any case, it makes a sturdy plant, and there is also a white cultivar, 'Alba'. There are also attractive purple cultivars among the low-growing spring-flowering phloxes, *Phlox subulata*, and the taller *paniculata* hybrids. The latter group includes the pale purple *Phlox paniculata* and the hybrids 'Otley Purple', 'Purpurmantel' and 'The King'. There is also a very wide range of white, pink, lilac, and red-flowered garden varieties of phlox. Purple cultivars of Michaelmas daisies are available too.

Hostas are grown not only for their beautiful foliage but also for their pretty flowers, which are often a shade of pale mauve.

Sea lavender or statice, *Limonium latifolium*, is a pretty sight in early summer with its cloud of little mauve flowers. It is rather unusual, and makes a beautiful alternative to the widely grown gypsophila. With their fine, branching habit of growth and panicles of little flowers, *Thalictrum aquilegifolium* 'Thundercloud', *Thalictrum delavayi* and its cultivar 'Hewitt's Double', and *Thalictrum roquebrunianum* provide a pretty contrast when planted among roses and large-flowered perennials. Their height varies from 80cm (32in) to 150cm (5ft).

The various ground-covering thymes are very different kinds of plants, and roses that do not grow very tall go nicely with them. White, pink, red and lilac to purple-flowering cultivars of thyme are

Rosa gymnocarpa, *a shrub rose which is very suitable for a natural planting.*

available. Pansies and violas come in a great many colours, including purple: some examples are the summer-flowering *V. cornuta* hybrids such as 'Admiration', 'Roem van Aalsmeer', and the purple-blue 'W.H. Woodgate'.

Purple-flowering annuals include the old-fashioned, delightfully fragrant heliotrope, *Heliotropius arborescens*, which can be placed at the front of the border. There are some very attractive purple-flowered poppies. Although it is not always easy to find just the right colour, it is worth trying to track down seeds of those garden varieties of the opium poppy (*Papaver somniferum*) known as 'Black Paeony' and 'Purple Paeony'. The various verbenas are very pretty, and an intense purple. *Verbena bipinnatifida* grows to about 40cm (18in) tall, *Verbena canadensis* to 30cm (12in), and *Verbena bonariensis* to 1.5 to 2m (3 to 5ft). The last-named in particular looks pretty grown here and there among other plants. *Verbena rigida* has a similar loose habit of growth but grows to only 40cm (16in). Finally there are annual pansies in many different colours, including purple.

A combination of clematis and a climbing rose grown as a hedge requires a considerable amount of care.

Pink with white, apricot or peach-coloured, purple and pink roses

Pink is another colour well represented among perennials. If you have a rose of a particular pink, and you want to plant perennials of the same shade with it, avoid giving yourself an unpleasant surprise by taking one of the blooms to a nursery or garden centre to see if

the colours really go well together. Michaelmas daisies, phloxes, erigerons and geraniums have all been mentioned under the headings of other colours, but there are plenty of them in shades of pink. The autumn anemone is an attractive late-flowering perennial. Some good pink-flowered cultivars are *Anemone hupehensis* 'September Charm', 'Superba', and the deep pink 'Praecox', *Anemone hybrida* 'Richard Ahrens', and the pale pink, semi-double 'Queen Charlotte'. Astrantias are available in white, very pale pink and deep pink, for instance *Astrantia carniolica*, *Astrantia major* 'Rubra', and *Astrantia maxima*. Most species of *Coreopsis* have yellow flowers, but there is now a pink-flowering perennial variety, *Coreopsis rosea* 'American Dream'. For the back of the border we suggest *Filipendula rubra* 'Venusta', a fine plant growing to 1.5m (5ft), bearing feathery heads of flowers. *Malva*, mallow, and *Lavatera* have the same shape of flower, in white and in pink. Mallows reach a height of about 80cm (32in). *Lavatera*, on the other hand, is an annual or sub-shrub. If not affected by frost or pruned back it will grow to 2m (6ft). The Greek mallow, *Sidalcea*, is a member of the same family, and very pretty, with white, pink and deep pink flowers. The cultivar 'Elsie Heugh' is a beautiful pink with a tinge of lilac. Although peonies do not flower for long they are welcome in the border and combine extremely well with roses, although the first roses are just opening when the peonies are

'Elmshorn', a shrub rose which sometimes has up to forty flowers to a cluster.

coming to an end. After the short flowering period, however, the plant is still attractive for its pretty foliage. A good pink-flowered peony is *Paeonia* 'Sarah Bernhardt'. The physostegia forms a sturdy plant growing to 80cm (32in), available in white, pink and red. A good pink variety is *Physostegia virginiana* 'Vivid'. Besides being a good border plant, it is useful as a cut flower. The pink *Potentilla nepalensis* 'Miss Willmott' is a lovely sight, but not easy to combine with other pink-flowering plants, being a very intense, cherry-pink shade. Recently a potentilla crossed with a strawberry has produced the pretty pink *Fragaria* 'Pink Panda'.

There are several pink annuals which look good at the front of the border, but not all of them can stand up to being combined with roses and perennials. For instance, the pelargoniums and begonias, which have a rather rigid habit of growth, are not so suitable, and we would advise you to plant something else. Try to find a few plants of clary, *Salvia sclarea*. This biennial has beautiful large grey-green leaves and pale blue flowers. The flowers fall quite quickly, but the bracts, white at first and pink later, lend the plant decorative value over a long period. Clary is quite robust and a good 1m (3ft) in height. Another very pretty plant is the spider flower, *Cleome hassleriana*. There are white, pink and purple varieties of this branching annual, which grows to 1.5m (5ft). Shorter varieties of roses can be planted in front of it, and its unusual shape would set

A particularly original rose pillar, shown with climbing roses and clematis.

them off to good advantage. Cosmea, *Cosmos bipinnatus*, is usually sold as mixed seed. However, packets of all-white or all-pink varieties can be found, for instance the pale pink cultivar 'Radiance'. There is also a pretty pink-flowered annual gypsophila, as well as the usual white variety. A sturdy, pink-flowered annual which also makes a fine cut flower is *Lavatera trimestris* 'Mont Rose'. Very different in size is *Polygonum capitatum*: not very tall, but extremely attractive. It is a pretty ground-cover plant with beautifully marked leaves, and is especially suitable for planting between small rose bushes, where it will quickly cover the ground.

Roses with red-flowered plants

There is not a very extensive range of genuinely red-flowering plants, since the red often tends toward either orange or purple. However, there are a few beautiful flowers of true red, such as the avens, *Geum chiloense* 'Mrs Bradshaw' and the rather similar cinquefoil, *Potentilla* 'Gibson's Scarlet'. Most of the knotweeds are white, pink or rose-pink, but *Polygonum amplexicaule* has red flowers. This plant is rather untidy in a formal border, with its loose habit of growth and long flower spikes, but it makes a good contrast in a more natural planting scheme. The campion *Lychnis chalcedonica* is fiery red, inclining to orange, and can find a place in a border in which orange is an important element. The coral flower, *Heuchera brizoides* 'Pluie de Feu', is a pretty plant for the front of the border.

Such a colourful abundance of roses is most suitable for a rosarium.

The fuchsia is a delightful bushy plant: *Fuchsia magellanica* 'Gracilis' is mostly red with a little purple "skirt", and is reliably hardy. There are also some pretty wine-red plants which can be used in a planting scheme with pink, purple and red, for instance the yarrow *Achillea millefolium* 'Red Beauty', and *Echinacea purpurea* 'The King'. The loosestrife, *Lythrum salicaria* 'Robert', has rose-red flowers, and 'Dropmore Purple' is a purple-red cultivar. Deep red accents sometimes look attractive in a planting scheme, and could be provided by *Knautia macedonica*. You might also like to consider red-leaved plants when planning your border, but do not use too many, or they will make the garden rather sombre. One pretty red-leaved perennial is *Heuchera micrantha* 'Purple Palace'. It flowers in summer, with little white blooms on graceful branching stems.

Bright red is a colour found more often among annuals than perennials. Not particularly familiar but very pretty is *Adonis aestivalis*, a small anemone-like flower set in fine foliage. There are a number of true red poppies, such as *Papaver nudicaule*, *Papaver glaucum*, *Papaver rhoeas* and *Papaver somniferum*. The seed of these beautiful flowers can be sown at random among perennials and roses, and groups of poppies will come up here and there, providing a natural effect. Genuine red is also found among the *Penstemon* varieties, but unfortunately they are not very freely

In a garden full of roses, the green of the lawn creates harmony.

available. The *Verbena* hybrids also have genuine red varieties, and so do the salvias, although we suggest you choose not *Salvia splendens* but the less obtrusive *Salvia coccinea*.

There are also nicotianas of a pretty red colour, deep red rather than scarlet. The sweet scabious, *Scabiosa atropurpurea*, flowers in lovely shades of rose-pink and red to purple.

White, pale yellow, apricot, peach, and orange roses with lemon-yellow and pale yellow flowers

Lemon yellow gives a sunny note to a planting scheme without being too obtrusive. Most of the yarrows are bright yellow, but there are one or two soft sulphur-yellow species such as *Achillea taygetea*. We have already mentioned *Anaphalis triplinervis* 'Schwefellicht' as an attractive grey-leaved plant growing to about 40cm (16in) and bearing pale yellow flowers. *Coreopsis verticillata* 'Moonbeam', also growing to 40cm (16in), is an excellent lemon-yellow flower.

A plant that does not grow very tall and is suitable for the front of the border is *Viola cornuta* 'Primrose Dame'. The taller bearded irises also include some pale yellow-flowering cultivars, such as *Iris germanica* 'Helge' and the sulphur-yellow 'Floriade'. Much taller is the yellow-flowered monkshood, *Aconitum lamarckii*, which reaches 70cm (28in) and often more. *Scabiosa ochroleuca*, which grows to about the same height as the yellow monkshood, is a beautiful pale yellow and is fairly unknown. It can be grown as a

'Bantry Bay' against the wall, 'Eyepaint' in the foreground, combined with yellow achilleas.

'Yellow Button', an English rose.

'Graham Thomas', an English rose.

biennial. We recommend *Kirengeshoma koreana* and *Kirengeshoma palmata* not only for their beautiful pale yellow, waxy flowers but also for their striking, quite large leaves, providing a quiet touch in the border.

Pale yellow annuals are not very numerous, but the beautiful pale yellow cultivar of the nasturtium, *Tropaeolum majus* 'Primrose Jewel', is worth a mention. There is a pretty pale yellow cultivar of *Petunia*, unfortunately not sold as often as petunias in other shades and colours.

White, yellow, orange, and orange-red roses with yellow to deep yellow flowers

There is a very large range of bright yellow flowers, in particular among the members of the Compositae family. Their striking flowers, often daisy-like in shape, are attractively eye-catching in a border. However, do not grow too many close together; a variation between different flower shapes will make your planting scheme more attractive.

Some good plants in this category are *Anthemis, Buphtalmum, Chrysanthemum, Coreopsis, Gaillardia, Helenium, Helianthus, Inula, Ligularia, Rudbeckia* and *Telekia. Potentilla* and *Geum* have already been mentioned among the red-flowering plants, but there are also several fine bright yellow varieties and cultivars of these species. Moneywort or creeping jenny (*Lysimachia nummularia*) and bird's foot trefoil (*Lotus corniculatus*) are attractive ground-cover plants, like the rock roses *Helianthemum*

'Golden Queen', 'Sterntaler' and 'Wisley Primrose'. Evening primroses have a number of pretty warm yellows in their range, such as *Oenothera missouriensis*, 15cm (6in) tall. There are also taller evening primroses, for instance *Oenothera tetragona* (35cm/14in), and its cultivar 'Fireworks', yellow with attractive red buds.

The golden rod, *Solidago*, comes in various shades of yellow. This perennial with its plumes of little flowers is a good cut flower, but some varieties need to be carefully watched when grown as garden plants, since they can spread rampantly.

A rather similar plant is the pale yellow *Solidaster luteus*, a cross between golden rod and Michaelmas daisy. Finally, among the perennials, we recommend the beautiful *Heliopsis helianthoides*, with cultivars in various shades of yellow. Although St John's wort, *Hypericum*, forms a shrub, it goes very well in a rose border.

There are plenty of yellow-flowered annuals available. Although African marigolds do not always look particularly good in a rose border, the roses themselves may be glad of their company, because they deter eelworm. Good yellow-flowered annuals that can be combined with roses are snapdragons (*Antirrhinum*), and marigolds (*Calendula*); marigolds come in orange as well as yellow. Then there are the chrysanthemum *Chrysanthemum segetum*, and the *Gazania* species, and you could grow the cheerful sunflower at the back of the border.

Following page: The rose garden at Sissinghurst Castle in Kent, England, contains a great many free-flowering old-fashioned roses.

Hips of Rosa nitida. *In autumn the rose combines attractively with red foliage.*

CHAPTER 7

ROSES

Yellow, orange and, orange-red roses with orange flowers

Yellow roses combine well with yellow- or white-variegated foliage.

We mentioned yarrow under the yellow and pale yellow flowers, and there is also a recently introduced pale orange cultivar, *Achillea millefolium* 'Paprika'. Also muted in colour are the pale orange to apricot-pink plume poppies, *Macleaya cordata* and *Macleaya microcarpa* 'Kelway's Coral Plume'. These plants, with their attractive grey-green foliage veined with pale orange, form a pretty background for setting off other plants, of course including roses. They grow to about 2m (6ft) in height. We could have put the foxtail lily, *Eremurus*, among the pale yellow flowers, but it fits in here among the orange flowers too, since there is a pretty pale orange foxtail lily of a colour tending slightly to bronze. This plant, crowns of which can be bought from bulb specialists, grows to 1 to 2m (3 to 6ft), depending on species and cultivar. *Eremurus isabellinus* 'Shelford Hybrids' reaches a height of 1.8m (5ft 9in). The plant has long, grass-like leaves, which start looking unattractive quite early in the summer, so they are best grown behind other plants which will distract the eye from their foliage, and their long flower spikes will then look attractive above the plants in front of them. *Potentilla longuei* is a pretty ground-cover plant with pale orange flowers that can be grown at the front of the border or serve as underplanting among low-growing and ground-cover roses. A brighter orange colour is found in the low-growing monkey flowers, *Mimulus*, about 30cm (12in), and the avens, *Geum*, which with its

'Rock & Roll', the Golden Rose of 1993.

inflorescence grows to 40cm (16in). *Euphorbia griffithii* 'Fireglow' grows to about 60cm (24in) and forms a nice, compact plant. You can find yellow, orange, orange-red and russet varieties among the day lilies, *Hemerocallis*, and a few that are pink to mauve. The grass-like leaves do not grow very tall, so the day lilies should be fairly close to the front of the border, but the plants behind them must not be too short, since with a few exceptions they bear their flowers on long stems growing to about 70cm (28in). The Inca lily, *Alstroemeria*, is better known as a cut flower than a border plant, but the bright orange *Alstroemeria aurantiaca* 'Orange King' makes a good garden plant too.

Plants with bronze flowers such as some cultivars of *Helenium* will provide a nice contrast among yellow and orange flowers.

Annuals are often very exuberant plants, in both their flowering habits and their colour, and there are quite a number of orange-flowered annuals that deserve a place in the border with roses. When we think of orange annuals, marigolds, African marigolds and nasturtiums are the first to come to mind, but there are others as well. It is sometimes surprising that certain plants are not in greater demand, and one such plant is certainly the orange cosmea, *Cosmos sulphureus*, which grows fast, is prettily branched, brightly coloured, and reaches about 1m (3ft) in height. *Tithonia rotundifolia* is not

'Bonica', a cluster-flowered rose.

81

Rosa setipoda, *a shrub rose, with striking flagon-shaped hips which go well with late-flowering orange perennials.*

Yellowish-green with all colours of roses

grown as much as it deserves either. It is a robust plant with quite large leaves, and flowers resembling a zinnia. These plants grow to about 1m (3ft) high. *Zinnia* itself also has orange in its range, but zinnias are not very often grown, and in an exposed position can suffer from the wind that snaps their hollow stems, so they should be placed in a sheltered corner. The Californian poppy, *Eschscholzia californica*, was frequently grown in the past but is seldom seen today: a pity, for the Californian poppy is a very pleasing plant, although perhaps rather on the tender side. The Iceland poppy, *Papaver nudicaule*, of similar appearance and rather taller, has attractive orange-flowering varieties in its range.

Recently the range of pansies and violas available has been greatly extended, and there is now a pretty pale orange variety on the market, *Viola* 'Baby Franjo'.

Plants with yellowish-green flowers combine extremely well with all other colours, which makes them almost indispensable in the garden. The most frequently grown is probably lady's mantle, *Alchemilla mollis*. This plant is very useful, not only for its greenish-yellow inflorescence, which can also be used as a cut flower, but also for its beautiful foliage. The lady's mantle grows to about 40cm (16in), and its cultivar 'Robustica' to 80cm (32in). There are also dwarf species such as *Alchemilla erythropoda* and

'Wedding Day', a very free-flowering climbing rose, with Clematis tangutica.

Alchemilla alpina, both growing no taller than 15cm (6in), while *Alchemilla vulgaris* reaches 30cm (12in) in height. *Euphorbia* too has some attractive and useful varieties with yellowish-green flowers. A low-growing species is *Euphorbia cyparissias*, which can still be found in the wild and grows to a height of 30cm (12in). Sturdier and rather taller, at a height of 40cm (16in), is *Euphorbia polychroma. Euphorbia amygdaloides* var. *robbiae* and *Euphorbia martinii* reach a height of 40 to 60cm (16 to 24in). Both these last two species are also available in bronze-leaved varieties, which look very pretty in a planting scheme with red or orange flowers. Also attractive, but not suitable for all soils, is *Euphorbia characias* subsp. *wulfenii*. This euphorbia grows to 1m (3ft).

Dill is a good annual. The flowers of this umbelliferous plant are often found as cut flowers today, but try growing it in the border, where it makes an airy, lace-like effect, and looks good among roses. The mignonette, *Reseda odorata*, has a lovely fragrance, and is an asset in the border for that quality if no other.

Besides the pink and red nicotianas there are some very pretty greenish-yellow varieties, such as *Nicotiana langsdorfii*, with thin stems bearing very graceful flowers, and *Nicotiana sanderae* 'Lime Green'. Unfortunately it is not always easy to get hold of these yellowish-green nicotianas, and you may have to look for a specialist nursery.

'Macblooba', a very striking rose, and difficult to combine with anything else.

'Golf', a ground-cover shrub rose which combines well with yellowish-green plants.

Roses in tubs and containers

Roses prefer standing in the open ground, but some can also be grown in tubs and troughs to bring colour to a balcony or terrace. The bigger and deeper your container, the more choice you have.

'Baby Faurax', a dwarf shrub rose.

Extra care Miniature roses (dwarf shrub roses) spring to mind first as suitable for growing in containers, but cluster-flowered and large-flowered roses that do not grow too tall can be used as well, and so can some roses grown as standards. However, there are several points to be observed.

First, plants in containers are much more vulnerable in winter because the frost can attack from all sides. Out in the garden, only the top layer of soil freezes, but the entire contents of a trough or tub can sometimes freeze to a lump of ice. If the soil in the container is very damp the roots, and most important of all the union, will be in severe difficulties. As you are not likely to have more than a few roses growing in containers, paying them a little extra attention is not a great deal of trouble.

The wind is something else which affects roses in containers a great deal, more than it does in the garden, especially if the containers are on a balcony. A first-floor balcony may be well sheltered by buildings, and tall trees growing nearby can help to protect it from the wind, but balconies on higher floors are a different matter. On balconies and roof gardens, wind can do a lot of harm in summer and winter alike. Not only can it injure the foliage and branches, but in hot summer weather it will also dry up the flowers, leaves and young shoots, and cold winter winds can have disastrous effects. So make sure the wind is broken by a light screen, for instance of

84

bamboo. However, you must also see that the roses are not in too sheltered a position, where pests and diseases are bound to strike sooner and spread more readily.

'Pink Cover', a miniature rose.

The right container

The material of which your container is made is not particularly important; roses can grow equally well in earthenware, plastic or wooden containers, so long as a few requirements are satisfied.

For a start, there must be enough room in the container for the roots to develop properly. The size of container will of course depend very much on the rose you want to grow in it. An ordinary cluster-flowered rose, or a large-flowered rose which does not grow too tall, will be happy with a tub of 10 litres capacity, i.e. the size of a normal bucket. A miniature rose, of course, can be grown in a much smaller container. Again, climbing roses need considerably more room; just how much depends on which cultivar you want to plant. Your best choice would be a variety that does not grow too tall, which will need less room than a strong grower, and in any case the space available on a balcony is limited.

Tubs and troughs have been in great demand in recent years, and the choice of containers available is steadily growing. New models keep coming on the market, not only in earthenware but in all kinds of plastic materials, and tubs and troughs made of plastic and fibreglass can sometimes hardly be distinguished from handsome

terracotta tubs or fine zinc troughs. Visit any garden centre, and you will find a very wide choice of containers in various materials.

Best known of all are terracotta pots, often imported from France and Italy. Terracotta is porous, which means that water evaporates quickly in hot weather and the growing medium will dry out quickly. In addition, terracotta pots are often less frost-resistant, and may freeze and break, particularly the attractively decorated containers. It is best to bring them indoors during the winter and store them in a frost-free place, or if you have a garden they can be buried in the soil. The pots themselves can be quite heavy, and it may not be easy to move them complete with their contents. So when you are planting your rose put it in a plastic pot inside the terracotta container, making sure that the edges of the plastic pot are covered with soil and out of sight. Then, when winter comes, you can just remove the plastic pot containing the rose from the decorative container and put the latter away. Another possibility is to pack the whole terracotta pot in hay or straw, or in newspaper surrounded by blister plastic wrapping. You must make sure the growing medium does not get too wet and let rainwater seep through into the plastic, but it must not dry out too much either. Glazed earthenware containers hold moisture in the pot better, but again, you cannot always just leave them outside in winter. Plastic tubs and troughs, which are much lighter, may blow over if they are very small.

'Kirsten Poulsen', one of the first cluster-flowered roses.

Other alternatives are containers made of wood, concrete or asbestos cement. In recent years the last-named have been manufactured without the harmful kind of asbestos.

Whatever material you choose, always make sure that surplus water can drain away easily. The best thing is to have one or more holes in the side of the container, just above the base. If the hole is in the base itself, it is a good idea to put the container on a couple of bits of wood or the pretty terracotta pot feet made specially for this purpose, so that excess water can run off easily. If a pot stands directly on a flat surface the hole is liable to be blocked and the water cannot drain away.

You can put a layer of clay granules in the bottom of the pot, to encourage rapid draining of surplus water. Choose pots which will not tip over easily; the straighter the sides of the container, the more stable it is, and the more room there will be for the growing medium and the roots of the rose.

'Little Flirt', a miniature rose.

Growing medium   The growing medium for roses in containers, just like garden soil for growing them, should be rich in nutrients. The easiest method is to buy some good special rose-growing compost and add some garden soil. The best time to plant roses in containers is the spring.

For the first two months the compost will still contain enough nutrients, but after that the roses should be fed every month, until

'Poppy Flash', a cluster-flowered rose.

about mid-August. When winter is approaching you should spread a good layer of well-decayed stable manure around the rose, just as you would around roses growing in the garden.

'Essex', a ground-cover shrub rose.

Watering The amount of water you give, and the frequency of watering, will depend largely on situation and the weather. Roses must never be left standing in saturated soil; the compost ought to be slightly damp all the time. On a balcony, even in heavy rainfall, the plants can get no water naturally, or hardly any.

When your roses have lost their leaves in autumn they will not need nearly so much water, and in winter water consumption is minimal. However, remember that the plants cannot be left entirely to look after themselves in open, sunny weather. Give a little water now and then to keep the roots from drying out completely, so long as the weather is not freezing. Do not give cold water from the tap (a good rule in summer as well as winter). As watering will often compact the growing medium, an application of organic mulch is a good idea, although of course it is practicable only if you are not growing any other plants under the roses. Both a mulch and underplanting will ensure that there is less evaporation during sunny periods.

Old roses and English roses

Old roses are in demand once again for their wonderful fragrance and the graceful shape of the shrubs. English roses are bred to display the best qualities of old roses.

'Rambling Rector', a summer-flowering climbing rose.

Old roses and English roses are very similar. The old roses of the past often have cupped double flowers with a beautiful fragrance, but most of them flower only once a year. The rose-breeder David Austin has crossed old and modern roses to combine the good qualities of both. His English roses have an old-fashioned flower shape, bloom all through the summer, and are often more resistant to disease than the old roses themselves.

'Kew Rambler', summer-flowering climbing rose.

Old roses
Most old roses date from the 18th century and were bred before 1900. Of course these old roses were not replaced by modern roses at one fell swoop around the turn of the century. The process was very gradual and included a transitional phase. There were already Gallica, Damask, Alba, Centifolia and Moss roses in Europe before the introduction of the China rose. Bourbon roses and remontant roses came at the beginning of the development of modern roses.

Old roses fell out of favour for many years, but recently they have been in great demand again, and they are available from specialist growers. These roses of earlier centuries have survived the passage of time and still attract us with their beautifully shaped flowers and lovely fragrance. If we compare the shape of a modern rose with that of an old rose, several differences are immediately obvious. The decorative value of a modern rose lies in the beautiful, slender shape of the bud. Once full-blown, the flower is often less attractive. The buds of old roses are often round as they open, with rather smaller petals in the middle of the flower. A full-blown old rose is a beautiful sight. Its shape differs from one cultivar to another, and may be globular or flattened, with many petals. The petals may be inward-curving, forming a cupped shape. Some flowers are quartered, with the petals curving from the centre at four places within the flower so that it looks as if the bloom were divided into four. There can also be an eye in the middle of the flower: a number of small petals at its heart forming a kind of bud, usually green. The colour range of old roses is not so wide as that of modern roses. They are often pastel-tinted, with pink as the dominant shade. Yellow and white are found even less frequently than red and purple. Unlike modern roses, old roses flower only once, with the exception of the Bourbon and remontant roses, which are almost always repeat-flowering because they have China roses in their ancestry. Old roses and modern roses also differ in their habit of growth. Old roses make rather large, dense shrubs with drooping branches on which the flowers are borne gracefully. If you want to grow old roses in your garden, you must give them enough room.

The description of each group of old roses is followed by that of a number of cultivars well worth growing. Where the dates are known, we give the year of introduction after the name of each rose.

A quiet corner in the rosarium of the Arcen castle gardens.

Rosa gallica *'Officinalis', the Apothecary's Rose. This rose was brought back from the Seventh Crusade by Thibault IV in 1250.*

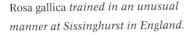

Rosa gallica *trained in an unusual manner at Sissinghurst in England.*

Gallica roses

Rosa gallica occurs in the wild in Central and Southern Europe. It is an upright shrub 1m (3ft) high, which makes many suckers and has branches thickly armed with thorns. The deep pink flowers have a diameter of 5–6cm (2–2½in). The small hips are round and red. Gallica roses have an older history of garden cultivation than any others. Over the course of time many crosses occurred. There were already twelve different cultivars in the 17th century, and by around 1800 the number had risen to over a thousand. Most of these cultivars vanished long ago, but the fact shows how popular roses were at the time. Gallicas are stronger in colour than other old roses, ranging from deep pink to red, purple and violet. There are also striped and streaked cultivars. Most of the Gallicas have double or semi-double flowers. Gallica roses form a small shrub of up to 1.5m (5ft) with coarse, dark green leaves. They have many thorns, and the hips are spherical in shape. Gallica roses were sometimes called French roses because of their popularity in France.

'Belle de Crécy' 1848

One of the most attractive and free-flowering of the Gallicas. The double flowers are deep rose-pink on opening, fading to purple later. The flowers open fully to reveal a green eye at the centre. The shrub grows to 1.5m (5ft) in height and 1m (3ft) in width.

'Belle Isis' 1845

This sturdy, dense shrub grows no taller than 1m (3ft). The double, pale pink flowers are not very large, and the branches have many thorns. This rose has a very characteristic fragrance.

'Cardinal de Richelieu' 1840

A shrub 1.5–2m (5–6ft) in height, with drooping stems, which needs fertile soil and must be well pruned. The flowers are worth the trouble. They are pale purple in bud, and as they open they turn a deeper purple and are globular in shape.

'Charles de Mills'

A very large-flowered Gallica rose. The blooms are double, and flat on top when fully open. They change colour from red to violet. This rose, which grows to 1.5m (5ft) in height, needs some support.

Rosa moschata, *a vigorous climber that can easily reach 10 m (33 ft).*

'Scharlachglut', 'Scarlet Fire', a Gallica.

'Conditorum'

A Gallica rose of unknown origin, with reddish-purple flowers fading to a paler shade. This rose may perhaps be identical with 'Parkinson's Hungarian Rose' of 1629.

'Duchesse d'Angoulême' pre-1827

The globular flowers are pink. The shrub grows to a size of 1m (3ft) in both height and width. There is some doubt as to whether this is really a Gallica rose.

'Duchesse de Montebello' pre-1829

The soft pink, double flowers are beautifully set off by the grey-green foliage. The flowers are cupped to flat in shape and extremely attractive, with a delightful scent.

'Empress Josephine'

A beautiful old rose, known today as *Rosa x francofurtana*. The old name, however, does the rose more credit, since the Empress Josephine adored roses, and in her time had the finest rose collection in France, in the gardens of Malmaison. The flowers are deep pink, with rather darker veining.

'Gloire de France' pre-1819

A low-growing shrub, spreading broadly, with very pretty double lilac-pink flowers. The flowers are pompon-shaped.

R. gallica officinalis, 'The Apothecary's Rose'

This very old rose is said to have been brought home in the 13th century by the crusader Thibault Le Chansonnier. It was grown for medicinal purposes, and thus acquired its name. This low-growing shrub has semi-double, deep pink to carmine flowers, which stand out prettily against the dark green leaves. When the rose is grown on its own roots it will spread quickly by means of suckers, and is suitable for ground cover. Grafted on an understock, a single shrub will grow to about 1.5m (5ft) in height, and the same in width.

'Scharlachglut', 'Scarlet Fire' 1952

This Gallica hyrid does not really belong among the old roses, since it is a modern hybrid. The flowers are scarlet, with a paler centre.

'Tricolore de Flandre' 1846

An unusual semi-double, multicoloured rose. The basic colour is white, with many streaks of lilac, purple and red. Grows no higher than 1m (3ft).

'Tuscany'

Another extremely old rose, described as the 'Old Velvet Rose' as early as the 16th century. The flowers are quite large, semi-double, and show golden yellow stamens at the centre. The colour is a velvety purple red. Grows to 1.5m (5ft). Like the Apothecary's Rose, it will produce many suckers grown on its own roots.

'Tuscany Superb' 1848

Resembles 'Tuscany', but is rather larger. It is probably a sport or seedling of 'Tuscany'. This beautiful shrub grows to a height of 1.5m (5ft).

R. gallica 'Versicolor', 'Rosa Mundi'

This rose resembles 'Officinalis' and is a sport of it. The habit of growth and abundant flowering are the same in both roses. The flowers are unusual in colour, pink with red streaks and spots.

Damask roses

Rosa x damascena is itself a product of crossing, but a very old one. It is thought that these roses, which were grown by the Persians, were brought home to Europe by the crusaders. They are supposed to have reached France in this way in the 13th century. The Damask rose is believed to be a cross between a Gallica rose and *Rosa phoenicia*. Damask roses can sometimes be confused with Gallica or Centifolia roses, but differ from them in having stronger growth, with drooping stems and larger thorns. The flowers are usually clear pink in colour and have a delightful fragrance. The Autumn Damask rose, a member of the Damask family, is a cross between *Rosa gallica* and *Rosa moschata*. It is of no interest in itself as a garden plant, but was probably the only continuous-flowering rose to be crossed with the old roses before the China rose was imported.

'Celsiana' pre-1750

This very beautiful Damask rose has large semi-double, soft pink flowers which open wide, clearly showing the golden yellow stamens. The foliage is grey-green, the height 1.5m (5 ft).

'Comte de Chambord' 1860

Really a Portland rose, but one in which Damask influence is obvious.

Rosa gallica 'Versicolor' ('Rosa Mundi'), a sport of 'Officinalis', interestingly streaked and spotted.

The flowers are double, quartered, and of a warm pink in colour. One of the loveliest and most reliably continuous-flowering of the Portland roses.

'Ispahan' pre-1832

Double, pink, quartered flowers, opening to a flat shape. Fragrant.

'La Ville de Bruxelles' 1849

Large, round, clear pink flowers beautifully set off by the light green foliage. Grows to 1.2m (4ft) in height.

'Madame Hardy' 1832

A real classic among old roses, and no wonder, for not many other roses can compete with the shape of its silvery-white flowers. They have a green eye at the centre. The shrub grows to 1.5m (5ft) tall and is very resistant to disease.

'Marie Louise' 1813

An old rose which flowers very abundantly. The flowers are large, double and rose-pink. Because the rather small shrub, 1.2m (4ft) in height, flowers so freely the stems sometimes bend down to the ground. The rose is therefore best trained over a low wall.

'Petite Lisette' 1817

A small, round shrub with small, double, clear pink flowers and grey-green foliage.

'Quatre Saisons' (*Rosa x damascena* var. *semperflorens*)

This remontant Autumn Damask rose has double, clear pink flowers. It is thought that the Greeks knew the rose in the 5th century BC, and it is mentioned by Virgil.

Alba roses, white roses

Rosa x alba is thought to be a natural cross between a Damask rose (*Rosa damascena*) and a Dog rose (*Rosa canina*) This group of roses is very old, and was already being grown by the Romans.

It grows taller than other old roses, to a height of 2m (6ft), and has white or pale pink flowers. The tallest cultivars can be grown as climbing roses.

'Celestial', late 18th century

This rose, which comes from Holland, has sweetly scented,

Rosarium of the Gasperpark in Amsterdam.

Above: 'Félicité Parmentier'.

Below: 'Great Maiden's Blush', an Alba rose.

Left: Roseraie de l'Hay, rosarium in Paris.

pale pink, semi-double flowers. The sturdy shrub grows to 1.5m (5ft).

'Félicité Parmentier' 1834

A rose with perfectly quartered flowers. They are a delicate pale pink when the buds open, and turn creamy white later. This rose is a good grower provided that it gets enough moisture in the soil.

'Great Maiden's Blush', 'Cuisse de Nymphe', 'Incarnata'

A graceful shrub grown as early as the 15th century. Double, pale pink flowers and grey-green leaves.

'Königin von Dänemark' 1826

One of the most beautiful of old roses. The warm pink, quartered flowers have a green eye at the centre. The shrub grows to 1.5m (5ft) and has grey-green foliage.

'Madame Plantier' 1835

A cross between an Alba rose and a Moss rose. A tall shrub with drooping branches which can grow to a height of 2m (6ft). Suitable to be trained against a wall or allowed to climb into an old fruit tree. The flowers are cream-coloured at first and silvery-white later, with a green eye at the centre. Delightful fragrance.

'Maxima' ('Alba Maxima')

This rose, dating back to classical antiquity, has been cultivated in gardens for centuries. A very strong shrub, which grows to 2m (6ft). Double flowers which open pale pink and turn to creamy white. A strong fragrance, like the other Alba roses.

'Semi-Plena', 'Alba Semiplena'

A decorative shrub with strong growth and large, almost single

flowers. This very fragrant rose deserves a place in the garden.

Centifolia roses

Centifolia roses (*Rosa centifolia*) are not quite such an old group as the Gallicas, Damasks and Albas. They were in their prime from the early 17th century to the beginning of the 18th century. At this time there were over 200 different cultivars. These roses were particularly popular with Dutch and Flemish flower painters.
Centifolia roses form rather untidy shrubs, but make up for it with their large, romantic flowers. Some of them need a certain amount of support.

'Blanchefleur' 1835

The only white Centifolia rose, with double, quartered flowers. The shrub grows to 1.5m (5ft).

'Chapeau de Napoléon', also known as Rosa centifolia 'Cristata', 1820.

'Fantin Latour', a Centifolia rose, called after the famous painter of flower still lifes.

'Centifolia' pre-1600

This very old rose is also known as the 'Provence Rose', the 'Cabbage Rose', or the 'Rose des Peintres'. It is one of the most beautiful of Centifolias, with pink, very fragrant flowers. The shrub grows to almost 2 m (6 ft) in height.

'Chapeau de Napoléon' 1826

This rose is also known by the name of Rosa centifolia 'Cristata'. The original name, however, is more appropriate. The exaggerated size of the calyx suggests the resemblance to Napoleon's tricorne. The rose is much the same colour as 'Centifolia', but not quite so deep a pink.

'De Meaux' 1789

A small Centifolia rose, 1 m (3 ft) in height, with small, perfectly formed, pink flowers. The flower is pompon-shaped.

This rose is extremely suitable for growing as a standard.

'Fantin Latour'

The flowers of this rose are pink, and reminiscent of the roses in old flower paintings.

The broad, spreading shrub grows to 1.5 m (5 ft).

'Petite de Hollande' c. 1800

A small bush, 1.2 m (4 ft) tall, with beautiful little double flowers in a rose-pink shade. Resembles the Centifolia rose 'De Meaux', and as the name suggests, was bred in Holland.

'Tour de Malakoff', 'Black Jack' 1856

A remarkably beautiful purple rose with large, cupped, semi-double flowers

The flowers display different shades of colour. The height of this shrub, at 1.8 m (5 ft 10 in) means that it can be grown as a climbing rose.

Moss roses

This group of roses (Rosa moschata) derives its name from the moss-like growth on the leaves of the calyx and sometimes the stem of the flower. The 'moss' consists of tiny glands which give off a resinous scent and feel sticky.

Most Moss roses date from the mid-19th century. The shrubs have an open, rather erect habit of growth, and bear hairy thorns on the stems. The flowers vary in colour from pink to purple.

'Comtesse de Murinais' 1843
A particularly beautiful Moss rose. The pale pink buds are covered with rough green moss and the quartered flowers, which fade to white, have a green eye at the centre. A picture of a rose.

'Général Kléber' 1856
The buds are covered with bright green moss, and when they open form flat flowers with backward-curving petals.
The shrub is bushy and grows to 1.2 m (4 ft). One of the prettiest Moss roses.

'Henri Martin' 1863
Semi-double flowers, carmine red fading to purple.
The buds are covered with green moss.

'Jeanne de Montfort' 1851
The long sepals bear a large quantity of brown moss. The deliciously fragrant flowers are clear pink. The shrub can grow to 2 m (6 ft).

'Mousseline' 1855
This Moss rose, unusually, has a second flowering period. The buds are covered with olive-green moss, and the cupped flowers are a warm pink.

'Nuits de Young' 1845
This deep-coloured Moss rose has small, velvety, dark purple flowers, and the buds are covered with very dark moss.

'René d'Anjou' 1853
The buds bear bronze moss, and the flowers are pale pink fading to lilac pink. The shrub grows to 1.5m (5ft).

'William Lobb', 1855
The reddish-purple flowers fade to lavender blue. This is a very strong, healthy Moss rose that can grow to 2.5 m (8 ft), and is extremely for growing as a climber through other shrubs or training against a wall.

Bourbon roses
These roses owe their name to an island in the Indian Ocean, the Île de Bourbon, now Réunion. The story goes that an Autumn Damask rose and a China rose grew side by side on this island, and a natural cross between them occurred. The flowers of

'William Lobb', a Moss rose of 1855.

Bourbon roses still have the character of old roses, but their leaves are already beginning to look more like the foliage of hybrid teas. In addition, almost all these roses are repeat-flowering.

Good pruning and sufficient fertilizer are necessary to induce the rose to flower freely a second time.

'Boule de Neige' 1867

One of the most beautiful of white old roses. The small round buds are carmine. The white rose that opens from them has backward-curving petals, giving it a globular shape. The shrub grows to 1.5 m (5 ft) and has smooth, dark green leaves.

'Bourbon Queen' 1834

The pink flowers are loose and cup-shaped.

The shrub grows to 1.8m (5ft 10in), and can be trained as a climbing rose.

'Commandant Beaurepaire' 1874

One of the three striped Bourbon roses. The others are 'Honorine de Brabant' and 'Variegata di Bologna'. The flowers are a shallow cupped shape, dark pink with paler pink and purple streaks and marbling. This Bourbon rose flowers only once.

'Honorine de Brabant'

This rose is paler in colour than 'Commandant Beaurepaire', and repeat-flowering.

The flowers are cupped, and the shrub, 1.8 m (5 ft 10 in) in height, can also be trained as a climber.

'Louise Odier' 1851

A strong, vigorous rose with deep pink, cup-shaped flowers. One of the best of the old repeat-flowering roses. Height 1.5 m (5 ft).

'Mme Isaac Pereire' 1881

A deliciously fragrant rose with very large cupped flowers, pink to lilac, which become quartered later. The rose grows to 2.5 m (8 ft). The second, autumn flowering is often prettier than the first flush of blooms.

'Souvenir de la Malmaison' 1843

One of the best-known of Bourbon roses, available as a bush or a climber.

The pale pink flowers are

'Bibi Maizon', an English rose, 1989.

'Charmian', an English rose, 1982.

'Louise Odier', a beautiful Bourbon rose, 1851.

displayed better when it is grown as a climbing rose.

'Souvenir de St Anne's' 1950

This modern Bourbon rose is a sport of 'Souvenir de la Malmaison', and has fragrant, semi-double, white flowers flushed with pink.

'Variegata di Bologna' 1909

A striped Bourbon rose, white with carmine spots and streaks. As a bush it grows to 1.5m (5ft), and as a climber to 3m (10ft). A rose of character, which flowers only once, and is unfortunately prone to black spot.

Remontant roses

Remontant roses are the forerunners of the modern hybrid teas. The group contains roses of different origins with the common characteristic of being repeat-flowering or remontant. Because these roses were specially bred for exhibition purposes, little attention was paid to the shape of the shrub, so that many of them do not have an attractive habit of growth. However, there are a few remontant roses that are still well worth the trouble of growing them.

'Baron Girod de l'Ain' 1897

This rose does have a well-shaped bush. The large, dark red, cupped flowers have a pretty white rim to the edges of the petals.

'Baroness Rothschild' 1868

Very pretty cupped pale pink flowers. The shrub grows to 1.2m (4ft).

'Frau Karl Druschki' 1901

The flowers resemble those of the hybrid teas, and are white. The shrub grows to 2m (6ft) and must be pruned if it is to keep an attractive shape.

'Mrs John Laing' 1889

The deep, cupped flowers are pink. This strong rose repeat-flowers well and grows to 1.2m (4ft).

'Reine des Violettes' 1860

One of the most attractive remontant roses. The flowers are double and quartered, with a green eye at the centre. The colour is velvety purple fading to a rather lighter shade. The shrub can grow to 2m (6ft).

English roses

Forty years ago the English rose-

'Fisherman's Friend', an English rose, 1987.

'Fair Bianca', an English rose, 1982.

breeder David Austin began crossing roses to produce a new group which he called English roses. Before that name was adopted they were known as Austin roses. He crossed old and modern roses to combine the good qualities of both groups. English roses thus have the natural habit of growth, the flower shape and the fragrance of old roses, and the repeat-flowering qualities and wider colour range of modern roses.

With a few exceptions, English roses flower all summer, so long as they get sufficient moisture and nutrients. The habit of growth of English roses is more shrub-like than that of modern roses, and so the method of pruning them differs from the pruning of modern roses (see chapter on Pruning).

Some of these roses, such as 'Constance Spry', grow so tall that they can be used as climbers. English roses look particularly attractive planted in groups in the garden. Unless the descriptions below mention that a rose flowers once only, it will flower all through the summer.

English roses which David Austin himself considers particularly attractive are:

'Abraham Darby' 1985
A fine, tall shrub, growing to 2.5m (8ft). The flowers are large, cupped, and apricot-coloured. A very strong rose which repeat-flowers well.

'Bibi Maizon' 1989
A graceful shrub with beautiful, cupped pink flowers and delightful fragrance. This rose does not flower freely until its third year.

'Brother Cadfael' 1990
The shrub grows to about 1m (3ft) in height, and has particularly large, soft pink flowers.

'Charles Austin' 1973
This strong, upright shrub has large, double, fragrant apricot-coloured flowers, fading to a rather paler shade with a touch of pink. Not entirely continuous-flowering, but will give a second flush of flowers in autumn.

'Charles Rennie Mackintosh' 1988
A very thorny shrub with dark green foliage, growing to about 1m (3ft) high. The cupped flowers are lilac in colour.

'Charmian' 1982
The dense bush bears large, rosette-shaped, warm pink flowers.

Above: 'Mme Isaac Pereire', a Bourbon

Below: 'Gertrude Jekyll', an English rose, 1986, called after the 'Grand Old Lady' of English gardening.

'Constance Spry' 1987

A shrub with a very strong habit of growth and beautiful warm pink flowers. It can easily reach 2m (6ft), and needs plenty of room. Trained against a wall, the rose can reach 4m (13ft). The flowers are very fragrant. Although this rose flowers only once, it is well worth planting.

'Cottage Rose' 1991

This rose flowers freely all summer, producing cupped, warm pink blooms. A very good garden rose to plant with "old-fashioned" flowers.

'Cymbeline' 1982

A shrub with arching branches and very pale greyish-pink flowers. It has a myrrh-like fragrance and grows to 1.2m (4ft).

'The Dark Lady' 1991

A rose with a low, spreading habit of growth and large carmine flowers with a strong fragrance. Height 90cm (36in).

'Emanuel' 1985

The large, opulent flowers are double and quartered. They have a strong fragrance and are a unique shade of pink with a touch of gold at the centre.
The rose is named after the famous English dress designers who designed, among other things, the Princess of Wales's wedding dress.

'English Garden' 1986

A pale yellow rose with rather paler petals at the outer edges. The rosette-shaped flowers are double, and very beautifully shaped.

'Graham Thomas', an English rose, 1983, called after the famous English rose expert.

'Evelyn' 1991

In David Austin's opinion, this is one of the most beautiful English roses he has bred. The large flowers are cupped and apricot-yellow. Very fragrant.

'Fair Bianca' 1982

The flowers are silvery-white and have a shallow cupped shape. There is a green eye at the centre. A very strong myrrh fragrance. Height 90cm (36in).

'Fisherman's Friend' 1987

The large, cupped flowers are crimson. Growth is very strong, but this rose can sometimes suffer from black spot.

'Francine Austin' 1988

This rose is named after David Austin's daughter-in-law. It flowers freely all through the summer, with clusters of small, silvery-white flowers.

'Gertude Jekyll' 1986

A beautiful warm pink rose with an intoxicating fragrance, growing to about 1.5m (5ft). Gertrude Jekyll, the famous English garden designer, would have been proud of it!

'Glamis Castle' 1992

A white English rose with a strong myrrh fragrance. It grows to a height of 90cm (36in).

'Golden Celebration' 1992

One of the best English roses with a delicate appearance and large golden-yellow cupped flowers.

'Graham Thomas' 1983

This rose is named after the famous English rose expert. The flowers are yellow, with a tea rose fragrance. Growth is vigorous, and the plant is 1 to 2m (3 to 6ft) in height.

'Heritage' 1984

One of the loveliest of the pale pink English roses. The flowers are borne in trusses, and the shrub grows to 1.5m (5ft).

'Jayne Austin' 1990

A beautiful English rose with shallow cupped flowers in yellow to apricot. The shrub grows to 1m (3ft).

'Kathryn Morley' 1990

A free-flowering rose with clear pink flowers. An auction was held in aid of charity to name the rose, which is called after Mr and Mrs Eric Morley's daughter Kathryn, who died at the age of seventeen.

'L.D. Braithwaite' 1986

A small shrub with beautiful deep red flowers. Height 90cm (36in).

'Leander' 1982

This very large shrub, growing to 2–3m (6–10ft) is one of the most vigorous of English roses. The apricot-coloured flowers are rosette-shaped and borne in trusses.

'Lilian Austin' 1973

Named after David Austin's mother. A shrub with a pretty habit of growth, and semi-double to double flowers. The colour varies from salmon pink to apricot.

'Pretty Jessica', an English rose, 1983.

'Shropshire Lass', 1968, English rose.

"The Pilgrim', an English rose, 1991. A favourite of David Austin himself.

'Lucetta' 1983
A well-shaped shrub bearing semi-double, pale pink flowers. It flowers very freely.

'Mary Rose' 1983
An arching shrub growing to about 1.2m (4ft), with clear pink flowers.

'Othello' 1986
The very large, cupped flowers are deep red when they open and turn to purplish-red later. The shrub grows to 1.2m (4ft). Rather stiffer in growth than most English roses.

'Peach Blossom' 1990
A rose that flowers particularly freely, with beautiful, quite large, pale pink blooms.

'Perdita' 1988
This small shrub, with an arching habit of growth, grows to 1m (3ft). The flowers are double and tinged with apricot. A strong fragrance.

'Pretty Jessica' 1983
A charming little rose, 70 cm (28 in) high, with warm pink flowers. Unfortunately it is rather susceptible to disease.

'Redouté' 1972
A free-flowering rose which makes a good shrub. The flowers are a very pale pink. The rose is called after the famous painter of roses.

'St Cecilia' 1987
A rose which remains quite short, with beautiful cupped flowers in a shade of pale yellow to apricot. Myrrh fragrance.

'Sharifa Asma' 1989
A small shrub with saucer-shaped flowers in a delicate shade of pale pink.

'Sir Walter Raleigh' 1985
A cross between 'Lilian Austin' and 'Chaucer', with very large semi-double warm pink flowers.

'Shropshire Lass' 1982
A once-flowering English rose. This healthy and vigorous rose grows to 2.5m (8ft) and can be grown as a climber. The apricot-coloured, rosette-shaped flowers are borne in large trusses.

'Sweet Juliet' 1989
Apricot-yellow flowers with a strong tea rose scent. The bush grows to 1m (3ft).

'The Countryman' 1987
This rather low shrub, 90cm (36in) in height, has an arching habit of

growth. The very beautiful double flowers are large, rosette-shaped, and deep pink.

'The Pilgrim' 1991
According to David Austin, this is perhaps the strongest of all the English roses. The pale yellow flowers are large, double and rosette-shaped. The shrub flowers freely, and grows to 1 m (3 ft).

'The Prince' 1990
This rose, which grows to only 60–70 cm (24–28 in) has deep carmine flowers which later fade to dark purple.

'The Yeoman' 1969
A compact bush, 1 m (3 ft) in height, with very fragrant warm pink flowers.

'Warwick Castle' 1986
The rose is called after Warwick Castle because a beautiful Victorian rose garden was laid out there in 1986, following the original design of 1868. The deep pink flowers are double and rather flat when open. The shrub grows to 90 cm (36 in).

'Wife of Bath' 1969
One of the roses whose names David Austin took from Chaucer's *Canterbury Tales*. 'The Prioress' and 'The Knight' are named from the same source. This rose, one of the first of David Austin's crosses, remains a fairly low-growing shrub at a height of 90cm (36in). The warm pink flowers are full and cupped. It has a strong myrrh fragrance.

'Wife of Bath', an English rose, 1969.

'William Shakespeare' 1989
A very robust and hardy rose, but unfortunately prone to black spot. The dark red flowers are rosette-shaped, with a strong fragrance.

'Winchester Cathedral' 1988
The flowers of this English rose are white, with a touch of pale yellow at the centre.

'Windrush' 1984
A rose which for once does not have double flowers, but large, single, pale yellow blooms. Height 1.3 m (4 ft).

'Yellow Button' 1975
The yellow, rosette-shaped flowers are quartered, with a green eye at the centre.

Shrub roses

Shrub roses make excellent hedges for which the birds will thank you, and you will enjoy the flowers and hips yourself.

The term "shrub rose" is rather difficult to define. According to some rose-growers and breeders, it covers all roses other than large-flowered and cluster-flowered roses, miniature roses and climbers. This rather negative definition can be changed to a positive one if we say that a shrub rose is a rose that acts as a shrub.

In the same way as large-flowered roses are planted for their flowers, shrub roses are planted for their entire habit of growth, flowers and hips included. Some shrub roses flower only once a year, others are repeat-flowering or continuous-flowering.

The species shrub roses (and their cultivars) used to be known as botanical roses. To avoid any confusion, they are classified as shrub roses today.

Species roses and their cultivars

The image usually conjured up by the word "roses" is of rather small rose bushes with large flowers, brightly coloured or otherwise. However, there is a large group of roses with less showy flowers but very strong, shrub-like growth. One specimen of such a rose in the garden is often enough, but it is useful to be acquainted with a number of these species roses and their cultivars. They can be grown in very different ways from the better-known large-flowered and cluster-flowered roses. If you want to plant an impenetrable hedge around your garden, shrub roses are very suitable as part of it, and the birds and insects will be grateful to you. Insects can take nectar from a single flower more easily than from a double one, and species roses also

Rosa glauca *making its way between an elder and a hawthorn hedge.*

make better hips than modern hybrids.

Many of the botanical species are suitable for hedges. For instance, the roses *Rosa canina, Rosa multiflora, Rosa nitida, Rosa rubiginosa, Rosa rugosa* and *Rosa virginiana* are often grown as hedging, either combined with other shrubs or on their own. Besides being described as shrub roses, these botanical or species roses are also called "wild roses" because they are species which occur in the wild somewhere or other in the world. Species roses have single blooms, flower only once, but make amends with their attractive hips.

Rosa arvensis, 'The Field Rose'
Forms impenetrable ground cover with its long, thin branches. Climbing into other shrubs, it can grow to 2m (6ft). The flowers are white to pink, and the hips are orange-red.

Rosa banksiae, 'Lady Banks' Rose'
Rosa banksiae occurs in the wild in Central and Western China. The small flowers are white or yellow, single or double. They have a beautiful fragrance and flower in May and June. This rose was brought to England by Robert Drummond in 1796 and planted in the garden of his Scottish castle. The rose did not like its surroundings. Scotland was much too cold for it, and it barely survived. Not until the beginning of the twentieth century

did a rose-breeder take cuttings from the plant and continue growing it in the south of France, where the Banksia rose was rediscovered. If you see a wall in a garden in the south of England today covered by a small-flowered yellow rose, it is almost sure to be *Rosa banksiae*. It can be grown further north and east too if situated against a warm wall and given some protection in winter, particularly while it is getting established. An English gardener has put it on record that in his youth this rose was protected in winter even in the south of the country. *Rosa banksiae* 'Lutea', the double Banksia rose, is the one usually grown.

Rosa canina, 'The Dog Rose'
This modest little rose is found in the wild in Europe. The shrub can

Rosa arvensis, the Field Rose, a shrub rose that not only has beautiful single flowers but follows them with pretty red hips.

grow to 2–3m (6–10ft) in height, and bears small, single, fragrant flowers in shades of pink varying from pale to dark. The hips are orange and egg-shaped. Since the shrub is armed with many thorns, the Dog rose makes a very good impenetrable hedge. It is much used as an understock. It is the native European species, and all ten different varieties occurring in the wild are found in the Netherlands alone. However, these wild varieties of the species are very difficult to tell apart, and the scientific nomenclature relating to them is very confusing, so we have not gone into the subject in detail here. *Rosa canina* 'Kiese' has single pink flowers and large orange hips. It is usually known simply as 'Kiese', since it is not certain that it is a hybrid of *R. canina*.

Rosa filipes

Rosa filipes is a very vigorous climbing rose that can easily reach 6m (20ft) in height. The shape of its thorns enables it to climb trees very well. The single white flowers are small and borne in dense trusses. A well-known cultivar of *Rosa filipes* is 'Kiftsgate'.

This climber is usually classified with the ramblers, because it flowers only once, very profusely, and has the vigorous growth that helps it to climb trees. The flowers of the cultivar are a little larger than those of the species, and are borne close together in very large clusters. Like all the ramblers, this rose takes some time to reach a good height, but if you have the patience to wait, it is an incomparable sight.

Rosa glauca

Rosa glauca was formerly known as *Rosa rubrifolia*. The special feature of this rose, which grows to 4m (13ft), is its brownish-purple foliage, frosted with blue, setting off the pink flowers and round hips, bronze ripening to red. The shrub has arching, red-brown frosted branches, and a graceful habit of growth. *Rosa glauca* 'Carminetta' has single, clear pink flowers and a great many red hips.

Rosa x hibernica, 'The Irish Rose'

This rose, now found only in garden cultivation, is a natural cross between *Rosa pimpinellifolia* and *Rosa canina*. It can grow to 4m (13ft), and has single, pale pink flowers and dark red hips.

Rosa hugonis

Rosa hugonis, named after the Rev. Hugh Scallan, is a rose of modest growth, 1.5m (5ft), with dark brown stems and single, sulphur-yellow flowers 5cm (2in) in diameter.

A special feature of this rose is that it flowers very early, often in May. The hips are broad and round, dark to very dark red in colour.

Rosa majalis, 'The Cinnamon Rose'

Possibly named for the colour of its red-brown branches. In any case, the term *majalis* refers to the fact that this rose begins flowering in

Rosa hugonis, *a free-flowering shrub rose.*

May, with single or double pink to purple-pink flowers. The long hips are dark red and smooth. The cinnamon rose is often planted by the sea, among dunes, and in such situations has gone wild and even become naturalized.

Rosa x mariae-graebnerae

An old (1880) cross between *R. carolina* and *R. virginiana*. The fragrant flowers are pink, and the shrub flowers over quite a long period. The red hips stay on the shrub a long time. The rose grows no taller than 1.5m (5ft). The foliage is beautifully coloured in autumn. This shrub makes a very good hedge.

Rosa banksiae 'Lutea', the double Lady Banks' rose, needs a sunny, sheltered wall as it is not fully winter hardy.

Rosa mollis

This rose, which is not very well known, is similar to *Rosa villosa*. Both have downy leaves.

Rosa moyesii

Rosa moyesii is one of the best of the hip-bearing roses. In autumn the large, deep orange, flagon-shaped hips steal the show. They can easily grow to 5–6cm (2in) in length. The shrub grows to about 2m (6ft), has rather small, pretty leaves, and single flowers in shades of pink to dark red. *Rosa moyesii* 'Germanium' does not grow quite so tall, and is frequently planted for its compact habit of growth, beautiful scarlet flowers, and light red hips. 'Nevada', a cultivar bred in 1927, has large, single, slightly double white flowers and dark hips. *Rosa moyesii* 'Ina Belder'

has very rich red flowers and a great many hips.

Rosa multiflora

Rosa multiflora grows vigorously and flowers early and only once. The flowers are small and single, borne in large clusters. The buds are tinged with salmon pink, and the deliciously fragrant flowers are white and followed by small orange-red hips. This rose's robust growth makes it very suitable for use in a "defensive" planting scheme. No dog would ever get through it.

Rosa nitida

A low shrub suitable for low hedges. The flowers are single and pink, and the small hips are orange-

Hips of Rosa filipes.

red. The leaves turn yellow in autumn.

Rosa omeiensis pteracantha (Rosa seracea var. pteracantha)

This rose owes its decorative value to its large, translucent, blood-red thorns. Prune carefully to ensure a supply of young thorns, which have the best colour. The single flowers are white and the hips almost black.

Rosa pimpinellifolia, 'Burnet Rose', 'Scotch Briar'

The burnet rose or Scotch briar is often planted by the sea. This attractive rose occurs in the wild over large areas of Europe and Asia. The burnet rose is a strong plant and will stand up to salty sea winds. The single flowers are creamy white, and the small round hips turn black. If you live near the coast you will

find this rose a rewarding plant. 'Stanwell Perpetual' is a *pimpinellifolia* hybrid of 1838. The double flowers are pale pink and sweetly scented. The small hips are black, like those of the species. Crosses between *R. pimpinellifolia* and hybrid teas produce attractive cultivars, with names often beginning 'Frühlings', meaning in German "of the spring".

Rosa rubiginosa, 'Eglantine', 'Sweet Briar'

Rosa rubiginosa has the pretty English name of eglantine, and is also known as the sweet briar. It is easily recognized by the scent of the leaves, which smell of fresh, sour apples. The foliage gives off this fragrance particularly strongly after rain. The flowers of this very robust shrub are rose-pink, the hips oval

Rosa multiflora, *with salmon-pink buds and white, very fragrant flowers.*

and reddish-orange, and the plant grows to about 3m (10ft). This rose is often used as an understock.

Rosa rugosa

Rosa rugosa is one of the best known of wild roses. It originally comes from Asia, but is now found naturalized in Europe too. Like the burnet rose, it is suitable for planting by the sea. This sturdy, strong shrub, with its rough, wrinkled leaves, is very often planted in public gardens and parks. The hips make excellent rosehip jelly. Rather less well known is the fact that Rugosa roses have some very attractive cultivars. 'Max Graf', an old trailing rose of 1919, has clear pink flowers and fresh green foliage. 'Agnes' has attractive old-fashioned

'Schneezwerg', 'Snow Dwarf', a Rugosa rose with semi-double white flowers and red hips.

'Sarah Van Fleet', a Rugosa rose.

yellow flowers with a beautiful fragrance. 'Schneezwerg' or 'Snow Dwarf' has an attractive habit of growth, with dense branches, and flowers all through the summer, with snow-white semi-double blooms. One of the best Rugosas is 'Roseraie de l'Hay'. The very large shrub, which can reach 2.5m (7ft) in height, is covered with very fragrant, semi-double, carmine flowers until autumn. This rose is a beautiful sight, and was bred in France in 1901. 'Sarah Van Fleet' is a strong shrub 2m (6ft) tall and 1.5m (5ft) across. The flowers are semi-double, cupped, and clear pink, borne in small clusters. 'White Captain', as the name sug-gests, has beautiful white flowers.

David Austin classes the Rugosas with old roses, like the Moss roses and Damask roses. In his opinion

the possibilities of this group of roses, from which a few cultivars were bred around 1900, have not been nearly exhausted. The above-named cultivars are in general classed with shrub roses.

Rosa setipoda

The single pink to purple-pink flowers of this rose have a scent of unripe apples, and can be borne in trusses of 20 blooms. The flagon-shaped hips are dark red.

Rosa villosa

This rose, found in the wild in parts of Europe, owes its Latin name, meaning "hairy", to the soft downy undersides of the leaves. A species rose with single, clear pink to white flowers, and large orange-red hips which ripen early.

Rosa virginiana

This rose is suitable for hedging, and forms a broad, spreading shrub with pink flowers and clear red hips. The foliage is attractively coloured in autumn.

The cultivar 'Harvest Song' remains low-growing, and has lilac-pink flowers and red hips.

Shrub roses, hybrids
Meidiland roses

The well-known Meidiland roses are good examples of continuous-flowering shrub roses. The firm of Meilland in France, which de-veloped them, calls them landscape roses, indicating the purpose for which they are intended. They make good ground-cover plants, have the characteristics of a species rose, but are continuous-flowering. They are much used in public parks and

Rosa rubiginosa, *the eglantine. The foliage of this shrub rose smells of apples.*

'Red Meidiland', a ground-cover shrub rose with trusses that can carry as many as 25 flowers.

gardens, but should not be regarded as exclusively for planting in public places, for they can also be grown in a private garden. They do need more room than we expect a large-flowered rose to occupy, and should be regarded more as genuine shrubs. However, they flower particularly freely and over a long period, and in addition are healthy and suffer very little from disease.

These roses are usually sold grown on their own roots, that is, they have not been grafted on an understock. The advantage is that they cannot put out wild suckers, the product of the understock, which have to be removed because otherwise they will impair the rose grafted on the rootstock. Beautiful examples of these roses are 'Pearl Meidiland', pastel pink with very broadly arching branches;

'Polareis', a Rugosa hybrid in a delicate shade of pink, a very bushy rose with slightly arching branches; and 'Red Meidiland', which has single red flowers with a white centre and striking yellow stamens. The flowers are borne in trusses of up to 25 blooms each. 'Bingo Meilland' has small, single, pale pink flowers with a striking yellow centre, and is suitable as ground cover and in combination with perennials.

Interplant shrub roses

The firm of Interplant in the Netherlands is another rose-growing firm which has taken account of the new trends in garden design and landscaping. At the end of the 1960s landscape designers began turning against the ever growing and ever gaudier range of

large-flowered roses. They preferred to go back to pastel shades, and roses with a more natural habit of growth. In addition, they wanted new roses to be strong and resistant to disease. It takes a very long time to develop a new rose, on average ten years, so a rose-breeder has to anticipate public taste. Shrub roses introduced by Interplant are:

'Chimo'

A broad, spreading shrub which grows to 1m (3ft) in width and 60cm (24in) high. The single, dark red flowers with their striking yellow stamens are well set off by the shiny foliage.

'Eye Appeal'

A low, ground-covering shrub rose with small, single, red flowers and sulphur-yellow stamens.

'Eyeopener'
A very free-flowering ground-cover rose.
Deep red flowers with yellow stamens.

'Fleurette'
A broad, spreading shrub, 1m (3ft) tall, with clear pink single flowers. This rose flowers very profusely.

'Pink Chimo'
Ground-cover rose, 50cm (20in high and 1m (3ft) broad. The single flowers are deep pink.

'Rosy Carpet'
A very strong, broadly spreading shrub with single, rose-pink flowers.

'Rosy Cushion'
An award-winning rose. Single, clear pink flowers on a broad, spreading shrub which grows to 1.3m (4ft) in height.

'Smarty'
A very broad, spreading shrub bearing clusters of white flowers with golden-yellow stamens.

'White Fleurette'
The trusses of single flowers are silvery white with sulphur-yellow stamens.

'Yellow Fleurette'
The single flowers are yellow and quite large. The shrub grows to 80cm (32in) high and about the same across.

Other hybrids
As well as the Meidiland roses and the roses bred by Interplant, there are many other hybrids which come into the category of shrub roses. These roses grow to 1 to 2m (3 to 6ft) in height and the same across. They can be planted among other shrubs. Most have single flowers, but some are double.

'Ballerina'
A rose with clear pink single flowers, white at the centre. Not very fragrant. The flowers are well set off by the light green foliage. Flowers through until winter. Can reach a height of 1m (3ft) and a breadth of 75cm (30in).

'Blanc Double de Coubert'
An old rose of 1892. A Rugosa hybrid with beautiful, semi-double white flowers. Very fragrant.

'Eyeopener', a ground-cover shrub rose.

Shrub roses with a box plant in a container.

'Golf', a ground-cover shrub rose with glossy green foliage and single white flowers.

'Bourgogne'
A robustly growing shrub rose with arching branches. The flowers are pale pink, and the flagon-shaped orange-red hips remain on the shrub a long time.

'Canary Bird'
A hybrid of *Rosa xanthina*. A shrub which grows vigorously, to a height of 2 m (6ft), and has large, clear yellow flowers.

'Cappa Magna'
Grows to 1m (3ft) high, a broad, spreading shrub with single red flowers.

'Frau Dagmar Hartopp', 'Fru Dagmar Hastrup'
A Rugosa hybrid with a bushy, broad habit of growth. The beautiful single, rose-pink flowers are very large and are followed by bright red hips. The rose grows to 1–1.5m (3–5ft).

'Frühlingsanfang'
A *pimpinellifolia* hybrid up to 3m (10ft) high, with large, clear yellow, fragrant flowers. This rose will flower for several weeks.

'Frühlingsduft'
A broad shrub up to 2m (6ft) high, with golden-yellow, semi-double flowers.

'Frühlingsgold'
A broad, tall shrub with single yellow flowers.

'Frühlingsmorgen'
A tall shrub 1.8m (5ft 10in) in height, with single pink flowers and a clear yellow centre.

'Frühlingsschnee'
A shrub rose with white, semi-double, very fragrant flowers.

'Golden Wings'
A tall shrub rose. It can grow to almost 2m (6ft) and flowers very profusely. The flowers are pale yellow with red stamens.

'Golf'
A new ground-cover rose with shiny, dark green foliage. The flowers are white and single, with a striking yellow centre, and the rose flowers from the beginning of June until the middle of October.

'Green Snake'
A very vigorous ground-cover rose with single white flowers.

'Hansa'
A Rugosa hybrid with purple-red double flowers and red hips.

'Immensee'
A vigorous rose with trailing branches. The small, single, fragrant flowers are pale pink. Flowers over a long period.

'Kathleen'
A rather tall rose which flowers freely, bearing clear pink flowers in large clusters.

'Lavender Dream'
Low, free-flowering rose with trusses of lilac-pink flowers. Height, up to 60 cm (24in). Bred by Interplant in the Netherlands.

'Maigold'
A vigorous shrub which grows to 3m (10 ft) and can also be grown as a climber. Bears large, double, clear yellow flowers. It used to flower only once, but will now produce some flowers later.

'Margaret Hilling'
The pink version of 'Nevada', with large single, pale pink flowers and red-brown stems.

'Max Graf'
This vigorous ground-cover rose has very beautiful clear pink, single flowers, and flowers only once.

'Moyé Hammarberg'
A very vigorous Rugosa hybrid. The flowers are full, fragrant, and violet in colour.

'Mozart'
One of the best-known shrub roses.

'Fru Dagmar Hastrup', a shrub rose with single flowers and bright red hips.

Bears large clusters of single flowers, pink with a silvery white centre. It flowers very profusely until the first frosts.

'Nevada'
A rose that bears large white flowers and flowers only once, although there is sometimes a repeat flowering in September.

'Nozomi'
A ground-cover rose with small, blossom-like flowers, pink fading to white.

'Persian Yellow'
Arching shrub that grows to 1.5m (5ft). Bears double yellow flowers.

'Pink Spray'

A very vigorous ground-cover rose. The pink flowers are well set off by the fresh green foliage.

'Red Ballerina'

Dark pink flowers with a white centre. Grows to about 80 cm (32 in) high, and the same across.

'Robin Hood'

Flowers all through the summer, with clusters of small, rose-pink, semi-double flowers. Suitable for a hedge.

'Rush'

The white flowers have pink edges to the petals and are borne in clusters. This free-flowering rose grows to a maximum 1 m (3 ft) in height.

'Sally Holmes'

A very popular shrub rose with arching, very free-flowering branches bearing single, creamy white flowers.

'Silver River'

A broad, spreading shrub with attractive and very fragrant little white flowers.

'Smarty'

A very broad, spreading shrub. Flowers very profusely, with large clusters of white flowers.

'Tapis Volant'

Gracefully arching branches bearing clusters of single pink roses.

'The Fairy'

Heavy trusses of small double flowers. A ground-cover rose.

'Weisse Immensee'

Exactly like 'Immensee', but with white instead of pink flowers.

'White Spray'

A white rose which flowers very freely, and only once, with a few blooms later.

Rosa moyesii, *a rose with very pretty hips, has single flowers.*

Climbing roses

Every garden ought to have a climbing rose. Climbers and ramblers look beautiful growing into a tree, covering a wall, or grown over a pergola or rose arch.

'Bobbie James', a summer-flowering, very vigorous and spectacularly beautiful climbing rose or rambler.

There are two groups of climbing roses: climbers that flower only once, and repeat-flowering climbers. The climbers that flower only once are useful for scrambling up trees, and the most rampant are also known as ramblers. In general they have more vigorous growth than the repeat-flowering climbing roses. They will climb an old apple tree or conceal a dilapidated shed. These tree-climbing roses take some time to develop fully. The fact that they flower only once a year hardly matters in view of the huge profusion of flowers they bear at that time. They usually have fairly small flowers borne in very heavy trusses. Repeat-flowering or continuous-flowering climbing roses include all kinds of different cultivars, with flowers either large or smaller, fragrant or not very fragrant, borne drooping or upright, and so forth. These climbing roses are best grown against a fence, wall or pergola. However they are grown and trained, climbing roses are a spectacular sight. Good pruning and proper tying-in will ensure profuse flowering.

There is an alternative way of dividing climbing roses into two categories, as large-flowered or small-flowered. However, the distinction between those climbers that flower only once and the repeat-flowering climbers is clearer, since it emphasizes a factor of some importance in the garden. Most of the climbing roses that flower only once are small-flowered, and most of the climbers that repeat-flower are large-flowered.

Once-flowering climbing roses

The once-flowering climbing roses, also called ramblers, form very long branches. When fully grown they occupy a great deal of space, not only in height but also in breadth. Most of the ramblers are small-flowered, but there are some large-flowered varieties, such as 'Albéric Barbier', 'Constance Spry' and 'François Juranville'. A number of very old roses belong in this group, for instance 'Adelaïde d'Orléans', introduced in 1826.

'Adelaïde d'Orléans' 1826

This old rose can grow to 6m (20ft), and is very suitable for an arch or pergola. The rose bears trusses of

'Bleu Magenta', a summer-flowering climbing rose that resembles 'Veilchenblau'.

'Albéric Barbier', a large-flowered summer-flowering climbing rose of 1900.

semi-double, creamy white flowers with a primrose scent. It is prone to mildew.

'Albéric Barbier' 1900

A large-flowered climbing rose which grows to 6m (20ft) in height and will flower again sporadically after its main flowering. The flowers are creamy white, double, and smell deliciously of apples.

'Albertine' 1921

A large-flowered climbing rose which grows to 6m (20ft) and bears occasional blooms after its main flowering. The flowers are a coppery colour fading to salmon pink.

'Bleu Magenta' c. 1910

A late-flowering climbing rose with some resemblance to 'Veilchen-blau'. The flowers are a beautiful

violet fading to deep mauve and grey. They have hardly any scent.

'Blush Noisette' 1817

This rose forms a rather untidy shrub 2.5m (8ft) high, and grown on a wall can reach 5m (16ft). The double flowers are lilac pink and fade to white. They have a carnation scent. This rather tender rose needs to grow in a sheltered place.

'Bobbie James' 1961

A very vigorous rambler which requires a great deal of space. Very suitable for growing into a tree. Bears large clusters of small white flowers.

'Buff Beauty' 1939

A shrub rose which can be trained to grow as a climbing rose. The leaves are coppery brown when they first

appear, becoming dark green later. The beautifully fragrant flowers are double and ochre-coloured. Grows slowly and flowers profusely.

'City of York' 1945

A rambler of moderate height, reaching 2.5m (8ft). Bears trusses of semi-double white flowers which have a very good fragrance. This rose will grow in shade.

'Constance Spry' 1961

The first English rose bred by David Austin. As a shrub it grows to 2m (6ft) and as a climber to 4m (13ft). The very large, fragrant double flowers are pale pink. Flowers profusely.

'Cupid' 1915

This vigorous rose, which reaches 4.5m (14ft), has striking flowers.

'Mme Grégoire Staechelin', a large-flowered summer-flowering climbing rose. It has large, double, pale pink flowers and large, strikingly shaped hanging hips.

'Leander', an English rose that can be grown as a climbing rose.

They are large, single, and pink tinged with apricot. The flowers are followed by attractive large hips.

'Dorothy Perkins' 1901
This tall climbing rose, which grows to 6m (20ft) flowers very freely with large trusses of small, silvery-pink double flowers. Prone to mildew.

'Emily Gray' 1918
A large-flowered climbing rose that can grow to 6m (20ft). The large, single yellow flowers are borne in clusters and have a delightful fragrance. This rose requires a sheltered position.

'Félicité et Perpétue' 1827
A beautiful rose, named after the two daughters of the gardener who bred it. Very suitable for pergolas and rose arches. It bears trusses of

quite large, double, creamy white flowers opening to a flat shape. Fragrant.

Rosa filipes 'Kiftsgate' 1954
An extremely vigorous rambler, found in the garden of Kiftsgate Court in Gloucestershire, England. This strong rose can reach 12 m (40ft). Bears large trusses of small, single white flowers. Small hips in autumn.

'François Juranville' 1906
A large-flowered rambler that can grow to 7.5m (24ft). The fragrant double flowers are salmon to apricot in colour and have a scent of apples. Suitable for growing on a pergola; not so suitable against a wall, because the rose is susceptible to mildew.

'Francis E. Lester' 1946
This rose can stand unsupported if

grown as a large shrub. As a climbing rose it grows to 5m (16ft). The small single flowers are pink in bud and later fade to white. After flowering, small red hips are formed in autumn.

'Gloire de Dijon' 1853
A large-flowered climbing rose with double, cupped flowers of a unique colour which could be described as amber, lying somewhere between yellow and pink. This is still one of the best of the yellow climbing roses. Very fragrant.

'Lady Hillingdon' 1917
A climbing tea rose with large, double, apricot-coloured flowers.

'Leander' 1982
An English rose which reaches 2.5m (8ft) and can be grown as a shrub or a climber.

The double, dark apricot-coloured flowers are rosette-shaped and are borne in large, open trusses.

'Lykkefund' 1930
A very free-flowering rambler with large clusters of semi-double flowers which open to a flat shape. They are apricot-coloured at first and later fade to creamy white.

'Mme Alfred Carrière' 1879
This rose, which can also be grown as a large shrub rose, has large, double, pale pink flowers. Flowers again sporadically after the main flowering.

'Mme Caroline Testout' 1890
One of the first hybrid teas, usually grown as a climbing rose. The climbing form is a sport dating from 1902, and is generally known as 'Climbing Mme Caroline Testout'. This rose is classified as a large-flowered, once-flowering climber, but it may produce some more blooms in autumn. The double flowers are a clear silvery pink, with petals that crinkle at the edges.

'Mme Grégoire Staechelin' 1927
A vigorous large-flowered climbing rose. Bears large, double, soft pink flowers. The flowers smell of sweet peas.

'Mermaid' 1918
A particularly beautiful single yellow climbing rose. This rose is not entirely hardy, and should be grown in a sheltered place and given protection in hard frost.

'Paul's Himalayan Musk'
A vigorous climbing rose which flowers profusely and can grow to 10m (33ft). The hanging trusses have small double flowers, pale pink fading to white.

'Paul's Lemon Pillar' 1915
This large-flowered, double, pale yellow rose can grow to 6m (20ft) and is very suitable for planting against a wall.

'Phyllis Bide' 1923
A large-flowered rambler which grows to 4m (13ft). The yellow to apricot double flowers have an excellent fragrance.

'Rambling Rector' c. 1912
A very vigorous rambler, extremely suitable for growing into trees. The

'Phyllis Bide', a large-flowered climber that flowers only once.

'Félicité et Perpétue', summer-flowering climbing rose of 1827, named after the daughters of the gardener who bred it.

'Flammentanz', a continuous-flowering climbing rose. It flowers very freely.

small, white, semi-double flowers are borne in tapering trusses.

'Sander's White' 1912
A vigorous rambler with glossy green foliage which sets off the clusters of semi-double white flowers beautifully. The plant grows to 4m (13ft) in height.

'Seagull' 1907
The semi-double white flowers, with yellow stamens at the centre, are borne in very large clusters. The rose grows to 4m (13ft).

'Thalia' 1985
The small semi-double flowers of this rambler are silvery white with a yellow centre. Grows to 4m (13ft).

'Veilchenblau' 1909
This small-flowered rose has a scent

of apples. The colour is very unusual: the small, violet-purple flowers fade to greyish lilac and have a white centre. This rambler should not be grown in bright sun or the flowers will fade too much. A position in half-shade is best.

'Wedding Day' 1950
A very vigorous, free-flowering climbing rose that grows to 8m (26ft). The single, creamy white flowers are borne in flattish clusters, and develop red spots on the petals when damaged by rain.

'White Dorothy' 1908
Large clusters of double white flowers. Flowers very abundantly.

Continuous-flowering climbing roses
This group of climbing roses flowers

from summer through to autumn. Some of these roses grow to a considerable height and have long, lax branches. Others remain quite short and have a sturdier habit of growth. Some climbing roses have large flowers borne separately, others bear clusters of rather smaller flowers. There is a climbing rose for any position; the possibilities are almost unlimited.

'Abraham Darby' 1985
An English rose which has already been mentioned in the English rose group. It can be grown as a climber as well as a shrub, and is often even more beautiful then, because the flowers tend to droop their heads and so look better on a climbing rose. The large, full, cupped flowers are a pale peach-pink to pale yellow.

'Aloha' 1949

This rose can be grown as a shrub or a short climber. As a climbing rose it will reach 3m (10ft).

'Altissimo' 1966

A shrub which is best grown as a climber. The flowers are very large, bright red, and single, with eye-catching yellow stamens. This cluster-flowered rose can reach 4m (13ft).

'Bantry Bay' 1967

One of the best climbing roses, a cross between 'New Dawn' and 'Korona'. The fragrant double flowers are clear pink.

'Blossom Time' 1951

A modern climbing rose with petals that are a deeper pink on the outside, giving this rose, which grows to 4.5m (14ft), its special attraction.

'Clair Matin' 1960

A climbing cluster-flowered rose which flowers very profusely over a long period. The rose grows to 3m (10ft) and the double flowers are a beautiful apricot colour.

'Climbing Iceberg' 1968

A very attractive climbing rose with clusters of semi-double white flowers and fresh green foliage. The buds are pink.

'Compassion' 1974

This large-flowered climbing rose is resistant to disease and bears fragrant peach-coloured flowers. The plant grows to 3m (10ft).

'Coral Dawn' 1952

A large-flowered climbing rose growing to 3 m (10 ft), with typical hybrid tea flowers, pink and not very fragrant.

'Abraham Darby', an English rose that can be grown as either a shrub or a climber.

'Dortmund' 1955

A climbing rose that grows to 2.5m (8ft) and bears large, single, carmine flowers with a white centre. The flowers are borne in clusters.

'Flammentanz' 1955

A modern large-flowered climbing rose. The plant grows to 3m (10ft) and flowers very profusely, with double red flowers.

'Frau Karl Druschki' 1901

A very old, strong remontant rose. The shrub, which grows to 2m (6ft), can also be trained as a climber. The flower is pink in bud, silvery white when it opens. Not a very vigorous grower, but quite hardy.

'Wedding Day', a very vigorous summer-flowering climbing rose.

'Handel', a climbing cluster-flowered rose.

'Golden Showers' 1957
A climbing cluster-flowered rose with sulphur-yellow semi-double flowers, attractively set off by the ochre stamens.

'Goldstern' 1966
Climbing rose with double yellow flowers which do not discolour as they fade. The rose grows to 3m (10 ft).

'Guirlande d'Amour' 1993
This new continuous-flowering climbing rose, bred in Belgium, is suitable for walls, fences, pergolas and arches. The small semi-double white flowers are borne in large trusses.

'Handel' 1965
A climbing cluster-flowered rose with double flowers.

The colour of the flowers is striking: white with a broad pink rim to the petals.

'New Dawn' 1930
A very strong climber with double, pale pink flowers. This climbing rose will grow to 6m (20ft) and can do well even without much sun.

'Parade' 1953
A climbing cluster-flowered rose which will tolerate light shade. The rose-pink flowers droop, and look best on a pergola or rose arch.

'Parkdirektor Riggers' 1957
This very strong rose has semi-double red flowers, grows to 4m (13ft), and can be grown even on a north-facing wall.

'Paul Noel' 1913
A short climbing rose, very suitable for growing as a weeping standard. The double flowers are apricot-coloured.

'Paul's Scarlet Climber' 1915
A very strong modern climbing rose that grows to 6m (20ft) in height. The red flowers are double, and flower until autumn.

'Pink Cloud' 1952
A modern climbing rose that grows to 3m (10ft). The double flowers are rose-pink. The plant flowers very freely and can be grown even on a north wall.

'Pink Ocean' 1980
A modern climbing rose with large pink flowers. The rose's alternative name is 'Havink'.

*'Pink Ocean', a continuous-flowering
climbing rose almost hidden by the large-
flowered clematis 'Rouge Cardinal'.*

*'Bantry Bay', one of the prettiest
continuous-flowering climbing roses.*

'Sympathie' 1964
A climbing rose with double, velvety
red flowers, 4m (13ft) in height.

'Zéphirine Drouhin' 1868
A Bourbon rose which grows to
2.5m (8ft) as a shrub and 4m (13ft)
as a climber. The double flowers are
carmine in colour. This rose is prone
to mildew and so is better not grown
against a wall.

*'Mme Grégoire
Staechelin', a
beautiful large-
flowered climbing
rose, has pale pink
flowers with a sweet
pea fragrance.*

Large-flowered and cluster-flowered roses

Cluster-flowered roses bear several flowers on each stem; the blooms of large-flowered roses are larger and double.

'Bellevue', a large-flowered rose.

Modern large-flowered roses were developed by crossing tea roses and remontant roses. The results were called hybrid teas. Today hybrid teas are usually described as large-flowered roses. The first hybrid tea rose was probably 'La France' of 1867. At the time this rose was regarded as a remontant hybrid and was not yet called a hybrid tea. Polyantha and floribunda roses come into the category of cluster-flowered roses. Polyanthas were developed by crossing remontant miniature roses with miniature China roses. These crosses were winter hardy, with small flowers and little fragrance. The polyantha roses were then crossed with hybrid teas and other forms of roses to obtain longer and more abundant flowering, and so the floribundas were created.

Large-flowered roses

The buds of this group of roses, formerly known as hybrid teas, are pointed, and the flowers are large. They are the roses we are used to seeing in formal rose-beds, and they have sometimes been called bedding roses. The bushes generally remain small and must be pruned in a particular way. Until very recently, more attention was paid to the flower than the habit of growth in the breeding of these roses. The fragrance of the flowers has also sometimes been neglected. Today breeders are trying to develop roses that have not only beautiful flowers but also a good fragrance, and are resistant to disease. A small selection from the immense range of large-flowered roses follows:

'Alexander' 1972

A strong, healthy rose with orange flowers that have a faint fragrance. They are borne on long stems and are good as cut flowers.

'All That Jazz' 1993

A new rose with almost single, semi-double, coral-red flowers. Its habit of growth makes it possible to classify it as a shrub rose.

'Alpine Sunset' 1974

Large bi-coloured flowers, pale yellow to pink, with a good fragrance.

'Bellevue' 1978

A strong, disease-resistant rose with yellow flowers. Good for cut flowers. It grows to 1m (3ft).

Large-flowered roses can have hips too.

'Blessings', a large-flowered rose with salmon flowers which contrast prettily with the red-brown foliage.

'Big Daddy' 1993

A new New Zealand rose, which as the name suggests has particularly large flowers. They are double, cupped, and orange-red. The bush grows to 1m (3ft).

'Blessings' 1967

The large, double flowers are salmon pink, nicely set off by the bronze foliage. A good cut flower.

'Chicago Peace' 1962

A very strong rose which grows to 1.2m (4ft). The large flowers are pink to apricot in colour.
This rose is a sport of the famous 'Peace'.

'Corrie' 1978

A bush growing to 90cm (36in) and bearing orange-red roses.

'Dainty Bess' 1926

A pretty single, pale pink rose. Very unassuming in appearance among other, more brightly coloured hybrid teas.

'Dame de Coeur' 1958

A rose bred in Belgium, with large red flowers. It is strong, healthy, and easy to grow.

'Die Welt' 1976

A bi-coloured rose, with petals yellow on the outside and almost red on the inside. The flower fades to pink.

'Dutch Gold' 1980

A bush with reddish-brown foliage and large, deep yellow flowers with a red rim to the petals.

'Eagle' 1984

A rose bred in Holland, with very large, dark red flowers. The bush grows to 1m (3ft).

'Ernest H. Morse' 1964

A fairly tall rose with light red flowers.

'First Love' 1961

A rose with pointed, pale pink buds, turning yellow later.

'Gisselfeldt' 1972

A strong rose with a rather awkward habit of growth. The flowers are dark red and make excellent cut flowers.

'Ingrid Bergman' 1984

Awarded the Golden Rose of The Hague in 1987. Velvety dark red flowers which stand out attractively

'Mullard Jubilee', a large-flowered rose.

'New Zealand', a large-flowered rose of 1991.

against the dark green leaves. It is essential to deadhead this rose.

'Just Joey' 1972
A rose with striking, large flowers. It begins flowering early and is one of the last roses to finish. The double flowers have fringed petals and are bronze in colour.

'Landora' 1970
A very strong, healthy rose with rather small yellow flowers.

'Maria Hofker' 1993
A Dutch rose chosen from Interplant by Maria Hofker on the occasion of her 90th birthday. The butter-yellow flower is cupped, and prettily set off by dark green foliage.

'Metro' 1991
An Irish rose, with creamy white,

prettily shaped flowers. The bush grows to 90cm (36in).

'Michèle Meilland' 1945
A tall, upright rose with large apricot-coloured flowers. Good as a cut flower.

'Monique' 1949
An old large-flowered rose, seldom found today, with beautiful pink flowers and a strong fragrance.

'Mrs Oakley Fisher' 1921
A rose with pointed buds and single, ochre-yellow flowers which fade to a rather lighter shade. Bronze foliage.

'Mullard Jubilee' 1970
A rose with large, dark red flowers and glossy dark green foliage. It needs some protection in winter.

'New Zealand' 1991
A pink rose growing to 1m (3ft). This rose was bred by McGredy, an Irishman who moved his business to New Zealand in 1972.

'Pascali' 1963
One of the few white hybrid teas, with pointed buds and medium-sized double flowers.

'Peace' 1945
This rose was introduced in 1945 on the day when peace was declared in the United States. Millions of plants have been grown since then. 'Peace' is the best known of the large-flowered roses. The large flowers are pale yellow rimmed with pink, and the foliage is glossy green.

'Peaudouce' 1985
A strong rose with large, slightly fragrant, pale yellow flowers.

'Peer Gynt' 1968
Very free-flowering, clear yellow rose. The flower eventually fades to a darker shade.

'Penthouse' 1991
A striking rose with bright red flowers. Its colour can be overpowering, so caution should be exercised in combining it with other plants.

'Picture' 1932
For what is officially a "large-flowered" rose, the blooms of this rose are rather small. David Austin calls it a "buttonhole rose". The flowers are clear pink and slightly fragrant.

'Poker' 1984
A Dutch rose with large pink flowers. In 1986 the rose won an award for the most fragrant rose in the Westbroekpark of The Hague.

'Polar Star' 1982
A free-flowering rose, white with a hint of green.

'Prima Ballerina' 1957
This rose bears large pink flowers, a darker pink in bud. The sturdy bush grows to 1m (3ft).

'Pristine' 1978
A pale pink rose of delicate appearance. A good cut flower.

'Red Star' 1973
A very strong, dark red rose. The bush grows to 1m (3ft) in height.

'Release' 1984
Forms a compact bush, with amber flowers opening to a flat shape.

'Silver Jubilee' 1978
A healthy, free-flowering rose with pink flowers, very well worth planting.

'Super Star' 1960
A good rose for cutting. The double salmon-orange flowers are well set off by the shiny foliage. The bush grows quite tall.

'Sweetheart' 1980
A tall rose with double pink flowers and good fragrance.

'Silver Jubilee', a healthy large-flowered rose.

'Peer Gynt', a large-flowered rose, opens yellow and fades to the colour shown here.

'Prima Ballerina', a large-flowered rose.

'Troika' 1971

A strong rose with large, orange flowers. The buds are dark red. Good as a cut flower.

'True Love' 1978

Bred in Holland, this is a double, silvery white rose. Good as a cut flower.

'Wendy Cussons' 1963

Large, striking pink flowers. The shrub is robust in growth.

'White Wings' 1947

A graceful rose with single white flowers, the red-brown stamens forming an attractive contrast. This rose needs a good deal of care.

Cluster-flowered roses

The difference between cluster-flowered and large-flowered roses is that cluster-flowered roses bear a great many blooms on each stem. Many cluster-flowered roses, however, do not have such large and double blooms as the large-flowered roses. Sometimes the dividing line is not clear; one grower will put 'Queen Elizabeth' under cluster-flowered roses, while another classifies it as a large-flowered rose. There is more variation in the habit of growth of cluster-flowered than of large-flowered roses. Height varies from 50cm (20in) to 1.5m (5ft). Cluster-flowered roses derive their beauty from the quantity of flowers they bear.

Among the Golden Rose of The Hague award-winners, there are five times as many cluster-flowered roses as large-flowered roses, showing how popular cluster-flowered roses are.

'Amber Queen' 1984

A very free-flowering cluster-flowered rose, in a rather unusual colour. The double flowers are apricot-coloured, and well set off by the red-brown foliage. The bush grows to 50cm (20in).

'Amsterdam' 1973

As the name indicates, a Dutch rose. The orange-red flowers are semi-double and the petals crinkled. The flowers look attractive against the darker foliage. 'Amsterdam' may need some protection in winter.

'Anneke Doorenbos' 1956

Another Dutch cluster-flowered rose. The large bush can also be grown as a shrub rose. The petals of the semi-double flowers are pink on the outside and white on the inside.

'Betty Prior' 1935
A cluster-flowered rose with single pink flowers. It flowers over a long period, and the bush will grow quite tall.

'Bonica' 1982
A rose that flowers very freely over a long period. Can be grown as a shrub rose and is also extremely good as a standard. The double pink flowers are borne in heavy trusses. A very strong rose, growing to 90cm (36in).

'Centenaire de Lourdes' 1958
A free-flowering, warm pink, cluster-flowered rose. Descended from 'Frau Karl Druschki'.

'Chinatown' 1963
A very free-flowering yellow rose which can grow to 1.2m (4ft).

'City of Belfast' 1968
A beautiful orange cluster-flowered rose, double, with crinkled petals. This attractive cluster-flowered rose does not grow very tall compared with some others.

'Coppelia' 1976
A Meilland rose with semi-double, cupped, bright pink flowers. It will flower freely until late in the year.

'Coventry Cathedral' 1973
A strikingly coloured cluster-flowered rose, its petals orange rimmed with red.

'Daylight' 1991
A Dutch rose with semi-double flowers, yellow with a touch of pink. The flowers look attractive against the red-brown foliage.

'Pink Parfait', a cluster-flowered rose.

'Diablotin' 1970
A strong rose with semi-double orange-red flowers and dark green foliage.

'Escapade' 1967
A very strong cluster-flowered rose that will bloom all summer, bearing large trusses of semi-double flowers, carmine pink with a white centre.

'Fervid' 1960
A single cluster-flowered rose with light red flowers borne in large trusses. Grows to over 1m (3ft).

'Fragrant Delight' 1978
As the name of this cluster-flowered rose suggests, it has a good fragrance. This free-flowering

rose grows to 1m (3ft) and has double, copper-coloured flowers.

'Freedom' 1984

A cluster-flowered rose sometimes classed as a large-flowered rose. The flowers are pale yellow, and the bush grows to 80cm (32in).

'Friesia' 1973

A short, yellow cluster-flowered rose with large, double yellow flowers.

'Iceberg' 1958

A very graceful cluster-flowered rose bearing double silvery white flowers. The pointed buds are pale pink. This cluster-flowered rose is often grown as a standard.

'Irene of Denmark' 1948

A short, slightly fragrant, white cluster-flowered rose. The buds have a tinge of red.

'Kirsten Poulsen' 1924

A single rose, dark pink with a white centre. One of the first floribunda roses ever bred.

'Lady of the Dawn' 1985

A cluster-flowered rose with double, pale pink flowers borne in large trusses. The rose grows to 70cm (28in) in height.

'Leersum 700'

A fairly tall rose with semi-double, apricot-coloured flowers borne in loose, flattish clusters.

'Margaret Merril' 1977

An excellent and fragrant cluster-flowered rose. Bears double white flowers.

'Maria Mathilda' 1979

A cluster-flowered rose with silvery white, semi-double flowers in beautiful large trusses.

'Memento' 1978

The double flowers are salmon to orange. The bush grows to 70cm (28in).

'Mountbatten' 1982

A strong, yellow cluster-flowered rose, which has won prizes in both England and the Netherlands.

'Nirvana' 1980

A cluster-flowered rose with very large flowers, semi-double and pale pink.

'Escapade', a very strong cluster-flowered rose that flowers all summer.

'Sexy Rexy', a free-flowering cluster-flowered rose.

'Orangeade' 1959

Unsurpassed as an orange cluster-flowered rose, bearing single flowers with a yellow centre.

'Pernille Poulsen' 1965

This cluster-flowered rose blooms over a very long period, with rather large, deep pink flowers. A robust rose.

'Pink Parfait' 1960

A strong, semi-double, warm pink cluster-flowered rose. The bush grows to 70cm (28in).

'Queen Elizabeth' 1954

Grown more than any other cluster-flowered rose in the world. It is sometimes classified as a large-flowered rose. The large pink flowers are borne in trusses on a tall, upright bush. This is a very strong, healthy rose.

'Sexy Rexy' 1984

A strong, free-flowering cluster-flowered rose with double pink blooms. The bush grows to 90cm (36in).

'Sylphide' 1993

A free-flowering cluster-flowered rose with small, double, ochre-yellow flowers. The bush grows to 60cm (24in). It was bred in Belgium.

'Bonica', a cluster-flowered rose described by Roger Phillips as flowering more freely than any other rose he encountered when making his television series "The Quest for the Rose".

Miniature roses

Some miniature roses must be brought indoors in winter and can then be put out again on a balcony or terrace in summer. Patio roses can stay outside all the time.

'Imperial Palace', a miniature rose suitable for the garden.

The smallest roses of all belong to this group. When they are suitable for growing out of doors they may be called dwarf shrub roses or patio roses, while those best kept indoors are also called pot roses. These roses are often sold as pot plants, and grow no taller than 30 to 40cm (12 to 16in). The flowers too are miniatures, no wider than 3 to 4 cm (1½ in) in diameter. The flowers of miniature roses may be single, semi-double or double. In fact miniature roses are not so new as is generally thought. Miniature China roses were introduced as early as around 1800. However, they have now disappeared. In the middle of the 19th century the dwarf Centifolia rose 'Pompon de Paris' was a well-known pot plant sold in the flower markets of Paris. In 1917 a descendant of the miniature China rose was discovered by Roulet in a pot on a window sill in Switzerland. The little rose was given the name of its discoverer, and called 'Roulettii'. Since then, a number of breeders have turned to the breeding of these miniature roses, among them Jan Vink, the firms of De Ruiter and Interplant in the Netherlands, Pedro Dot in Spain, and Ralph Moore in America. Interplant is steadily producing new miniature roses, including 'Suntan', with semi-double flowers the shade of a sun-tanned skin.

Ralph Moore, who has been occupied with the crossing of roses for over sixty-five years, has introduced miniature roses reminiscent of Moss roses, such as the red 'Scarlet Moss'.

Miniature roses treated as pot plants are usually regarded as annuals. Many of them are not hardy, but others can perfectly well be put out in the garden. There is much confusion of names in the world of miniature roses. Some rose-growers have given up and simply offer miniature roses for sale by colour. Certain breeders have tried to bring order to the chaos by adding a prefix or suffix to the names of their roses. For instance, miniature roses with the words 'Hit' and 'Parade' in their variety names are suitable for use indoors, while roses whose names include the words 'Cover' ('Easy Cover', 'Gentle Cover', 'Pink Cover' and 'Sun Cover') and 'Palace' ('Hampton Palace', 'Imperial Palace', 'Topkapi Palace') are suitable for growing out of doors.

The miniature roses sold as indoor pot plants can also brighten up a terrace or balcony when grown as annuals in a container.

Size of flower and bush is not always constant among miniature roses suitable for growing outside. For instance, some growers will place the rose 'The Fairy' in the miniature rose category, while others will classify it as a ground-cover rose.

The following miniature or dwarf shrub roses are genuine garden roses that can be grown either in the border or in pots and troughs, and are fully winter hardy.

Miniature roses in a bedding scheme to look like wedges of tart, in the Plantarium, Boskoop, Holland.

'Sun Cover', often sold as a pot plant, can be grown out of doors as well.

'Gentle Cover', a miniature rose, can be planted in the border.

'Bayernland Cover', a prettily coloured miniature rose.

'Cinderella' 1975
Very small, double, pale pink flowers.

'Elegant Pearl' 1984
Large clusters of single, creamy white flowers. The little bushes grow to 40cm (16in).

'Finnstar' 1979
Double to semi-double orange flowers.

'Fresh Pink' 1964
Double, pale pink flowers in large trusses.

'Lia' 1992
One of the new miniature roses from Interplant, with semi-double orange flowers and beautiful dark foliage.

'Little Flirt'
Semi-double, pale red with yellow.

'Magic Carousel' 1972
A bi-coloured rose, white with a rose-red edge to the petals.

'Minirette' 1981
Semi-double, pale pink miniature rose with beautiful shiny green foliage.

'Mr Bluebird' 1960
Pink to lavender-blue miniature rose.

'Petit Four' 1981
Semi-double, light pink to dark pink flowers, and glossy green foliage.

'Pink Reflection' 1979
Despite its name, a miniature rose with white to creamy yellow flowers and clearly visible stamens.

'Robin Redbreast' 1985
This little rose does its name credit, bearing clusters of clear red flowers with a white centre.

'Suntan' 1991
Semi-double flowers of a "sun-tanned" colour.

'Twinkle' 1989
Quite large double yellow flowers. The bush grows no taller than 30cm (12in).

'Zwergkönig' 1980
Double, dark red flowers.

Standard roses

Large-flowered roses, cluster-flowered roses, climbing roses, continuous-flowering shrub roses, English roses and miniature roses can all be grown as standards.

'Maria Mathilda', a white cluster-flowered rose, grown as a standard.

There is only a limited number of standards from each group on the market. The height of the stem differs; for a cluster-flowered rose grown as a standard, for instance, it is 80cm (32in) and for a climbing rose 1.25m (4ft). A climbing rose grown as a standard is described as a weeping standard. The rose used for grafting, which forms the head of the standard, is not the same as the understock. The desired rose is grafted on the understock at least three times, to create a beautifully and regularly shaped standard rose.

Standard roses can also be used to very good effect in a small garden. Combined with suitable underplanting (see Chapter 7) they can produce a pretty overall effect. Standard roses give the garden a romantic atmosphere reminiscent of earlier times. They fit well into designs for formal gardens, surrounded by box hedging.
Every standard rose needs to be tied to a stout stake. There is a great deal of work for a grower in growing standard roses, so the price is higher than the price of ordinary roses. If you want a standard rose you must be sure you realize that it will need more care than other roses, for instance very careful pruning, and you must protect the union in winter.

Some attractive roses from each group suitable for growing as standards are listed below, arranged by colour. Only the colour and the name of the group are given. Further information will be found in

'Ballerina', a shrub rose which can be grown as a standard.

'Lavender Dream', a free-flowering shrub rose, makes a good standard.

Top: 'Metro', a large-flowered white rose which can be grown as a standard.

the descriptions of the roses under their own groups in the preceding chapters.

White standard roses

'Elegant Pearl'
– miniature rose
'Guirlande d'Amour'
– climbing rose (weeping standard)
'Iceberg'
– cluster-flowered rose
'Margaret Merril'
– cluster-flowered rose
'Maria Mathilda'
– cluster-flowered rose
'Pascali'
– large-flowered rose
'Polar Star'
– large-flowered rose
'Rush'
– continuous-flowering shrub rose,
white with pink edging
'Sander's White'
– climbing rose (weeping standard)
'True Love'
– large-flowered rose
'White Dorothy'
– climbing rose (weeping standard)
'White Fleurette'
– continuous-flowering shrub rose

Yellow and apricot standard roses

'Abraham Darby'
– English rose
'Amber Queen'
– cluster-flowered rose
'Daylight'
– cluster-flowered rose
'Fragrant Delight'
– coppery cluster-flowered rose
'Freedom'
– cluster-flowered rose
'Just Joey'
– large-flowered bronze rose

'Landora'
– large-flowered rose
'Leersum 700'
– cluster-flowered rose
'Maria Hofker'
– large-flowered rose
'Peace'
– large-flowered rose
'Peaudouce'
– large-flowered rose
'Peer Gynt'
– large-flowered rose
'Release'
– large-flowered rose, amber-
coloured
'Suntan'
– miniature rose
'Troika'
– large-flowered copper rose
'Twinkle'
– miniature rose
'Yellow Fleurette'
– shrub rose

Pink standard roses

'Ballerina'
– shrub rose
'Blessings'
– large-flowered salmon rose
'Bonica'
– cluster-flowered rose
'Dorothy Perkins'
– climbing rose (weeping standard)
'Fleurette'
– shrub rose
'Heritage'
– English rose
'Immensee'
– shrub rose
'Lavender Dream'
– lilac-pink shrub rose
'Mary Rose'
– English rose
'Mullard Jubilee'
– dark red large-flowered rose
'New Dawn'
– climbing rose (weeping standard)

'Nozomi'
– shrub rose
'Penthouse'
– large-flowered rose
'Pernille Poulsen'
– dark red cluster-flowered rose
'Queen Elizabeth'
– cluster-flowered rose
'Tapis Volant'
– shrub rose
'Wendy Cussons'
– fuchsia-pink large-flowered rose

Red (and some orange) standard roses

'Alexander'
– orange large-flowered rose
'Big Daddy'
– orange large-flowered rose
'Chimo'
– shrub rose
'Dame de Coeur'
– large-flowered rose

A very large-flowered rose, an impressive sight grown as a standard.

'Diablotin'
– orange-red cluster-flowered rose
'Gisselfeldt'
– large-flowered rose
'Ingrid Bergman'
– large-flowered rose
'Memento'
– cluster-flowered rose
'Parkdirektor Riggers'
– climbing rose (weeping standard)
'Robin Redbreast'
– miniature rose
'Zwergkönig'
– miniature rose

Useful addresses

In the United Kingdom:

The Royal National Rose Society
Chiswell Green
St Albans
Herts
AL2 3NR

The Royal Horticultural Society
80 Vincent Square
London SW1P 2PE

David Austin Roses
Bowling Green Lane
Allbrighton
Wolverhampton
WV7 3HB

Peter Beales Roses
London Road
Attleborough
Norfolk
NR17 1AY

Cants of Colchester Ltd
Nayland Road
Mile End
Colchester
Essex
CO4 5EB

R. Harkness & Co Ltd.
The Rose Gardens
Cambridge Road
Hitchin
Herts
SG4 0JT

In the United States:

American Rose Society
PO Box 30000
Shreveport, LA 71130-0030

Seeds of plants suitable for growing with roses may be obtained from:

Suttons Seeds Ltd
Hele Road
Torquay
Devon TQ2 7QJ

Thompson & Morgan
Poplar Lane
Ipswich
Suffolk IP8 3BU

Unwins Seeds Ltd
Impington Lane
Histon
Cambridge CB4 4ZZ

Rose gardens to visit:

David Austin Roses (plant centre and rose gardens)
Bowling Green Lane
Albrighton
Wolverhampton
WV7 3HB

Peter Beales Roses
Attleborough
Norfolk
NR17 1AY

and at:

Mannington Gardens
Mannington Hall
Saxthorpe
Norwich NR11 7BB

Gardens of the Rose (Royal National Rose Society)
Chiswell Green
St Albans
Herts

Gardens of the Royal Horticultural Society
Wisley Gardens
Ripley
Surrey

Queen Mary Rose Gardens
Regents Park
London

Brooklyn Botanic Garden
1000 Washington Avenue
Brooklyn, NY 11225

New York Botanical Garden
Southern Boulevard & 200th Street
Bronx, NY 10438

The International Rose Test Gardens
Washington Park
Portland, OR

Bibliography

Old Roses and English Roses,
David Austin, London, Antique Collectors Club, 1992.
Shrub Roses and Climbing Roses, with Hybrid Tea and Floribunda Roses,
David Austin, Woodbridge, Antique Collectors Club, 1993.
David Austin's English Roses,
David Austin, London, Conran Octopus, 1993.
Roses,
Peter Beales, London, Harvill, 1992.
Modern Garden Roses,
Peter Harkness, London, Cassell, 1990.
The Complete Book of Roses,
John Mattock, London, Ward Lock, 1994.
Roses,
Roger Phillips and Martyn Rix, London, Pan, 1988.
The Quest for the Rose,
Roger Phillips and Martyn Rix, London, BBC Books, 1993.
The Redouté Album,
Martyn Rix and Alison Rix, London, Studio Editions, 1990.

Photographic credits

Index

Acer campestre 54
achillea 75
Achillea millefolium 'Paprika' 80
Achillea millefolium
    'Red Beauty' 74
Achillea millefolium
    'Schwefelblüte' 63
Achillea taygetea 75
Aconitum cammarum
    'Bressingham Spire' 67
Aconitum carmichaelii 66
Aconitum henryi 'Spark' 67
Aconitum lamarckii 75
Actinidia kolomikta 68
Adonis aestivalis 74
African marigold 77
Ageratum 65
Alchemilla alpina 82
Alchemilla erythropoda 82
Alchemilla mollis 82
Alchemilla mollis 'Robustica' 82
Alchemilla vulgaris 83
Alstroemeria aurantiaca
    'Orange King' 81
Anaphalis triplinervis 63
Anaphalis triplinervis
    'Schwefellicht' 63
Anemone hupehensis 'Praecox' 71
Anemone hupehensis
    'September Charm' 71
Anemone hupehensis 'Superba' 71
Anemone hybrida
    'Queen Charlotte' 71
Anemone hybrida
    'Richard Ahrens' 71
Anthemis 76
Antirrhinum 77
Artemisia schmidtiana 'Nana' 63
Artemisia stelleriana 63
Aster novi-belgii 'Audrey' 64
Aster novi-belgii 'Plenty' 64
astrantia 71
Astrantia carniolica 71
Astrantia major 'Rubra' 71
Astrantia maxima 71
avens 80

bearded iris 66
Berberis buxifolia 'Nana' 44
Berberis thunbergii
    'Atropurpurea Nana' 44
Berberis thunbergii 'Kobold' 44
beech 55
Bird's foot trefoil 76
Blackthorn 55
Bourbon roses 97
Brachycome 65
Buphtalmum 76
Buxus 44

Calendula 77
Californian poppy 82
catmint 65

Campanula carpatica 67
Campanula carpatica
    'Blue Chips' 67
Campanula glomerata 'Alba' 68
Campanula glomerata 'Superba' 68
Campanula lactiflora 64, 67
Campanula persicifolia
    'Coerulea' 64
Campanula poscharskyana 67
Carpinus betulus 55
Caryopteris clandonensis 65
Centaurea cineraria 65
Cerastium biebersteinii 63
Chinese roses 9
chrysanthemum 76
Chrysanthemum segetum 77
Clematis bonstedtii
    'Crépuscule' 67
Clematis durandii 67
Clematis heracleifolia
    'Côte d'Azur' 67
Clematis integrifolia 67
Clematis 'Lord Nevill' 66
Clematis 'The President' 42
Clematis tangutica 82
Cleome hassleriana 72
cluster-flowered roses 130
Coreopsis rosea
    'American Dream' 71
Coreopsis verticillata
    'Moonbeam' 75
cornel cherry 55
Cornus mas 55
Corylus avellana 55
cosmea 72, 81
Cosmos bipinnatus 'Radiance' 72
Cosmos sulphureus 81
Crataegus monogyna 54

day lily 81
delphinium 65
Delphinium 'Clivedon Beauty' 65
Delphinium 'Crown Jewel' 65
Delphinium 'Gletscherwasser' 65
Delphinium 'Loch Leven' 65
Dianthus plumaris 63
Didiscus caeruleus 68
dill 83
Dog rose 8

Echinacea purpurea 'The King' 74
Echinops 64
eglantine 9
English roses 99
Eremurus isabellinus
    'Shelford Hybrids' 80
Erigeron 64
Erigeron 'Shining Sea' 64
Eryngium 64
Eschscholzia californica 82
euphorbia 81
Euphorbia amygdaloides
    var. robbiae 83
Euphorbia characias subsp.
    wulfenii 83
Euphorbia cyparissias 83
Euphorbia griffithii 'Fireglow' 80
Euphorbia martinii 83
Euphorbia polychroma 83

Fagus sylvatica 55
Felicia 65
Filipendula rubra 'Venusta' 71
flax 65
fleabane 64
foxtail lily 80
Fragaria 'Pink Panda' 72
Fuchsia magellanica 'Gracilis' 74

Gaillardia 76
Gazania 77
Geranium sylvaticum
    'Mayflower' 64
Geum 76, 80
Geum chiloense 'Mrs Bradshaw' 73
globe thistle 64
golden rod 77
Greek mallow 71
gypsophila 66
Gypsophila repens 66

hawthorn 55
hazel 55
hedge maple 54
Helenium 76, 81
Helianthemum 'Golden Queen' 76
Helianthemum 'Sterntaler' 76
Helianthemum
    'Wisley Primrose' 76
Helianthus 76
Heliopsis helianthoides 77
Heliotropius arborescens 70
heliotrope 70
Hemerocallis 81
Heuchera brizoides
    'Pluie de Feu' 73
Heuchera micrantha
    'Purple Palace' 74
holly 55
hornbeam 55
Hosta fortunei 'Hyacinthina' 64
Hosta sieboldiana 'Elegans' 64
Hosta tardiana 'Halcyon' 64
Hypericum 77
hyssop 67
Hyssopus officinalis 67

Iceland poppy 82
Inca lily 81
Inula 76
Iris germanica 'Floriade' 75
Iris germanica 'Helge' 75
Iris germanica hybrids 66

Jacob's ladder 65

Kirengeshoma koreana 75
Kirengeshoma palmata 76
Knautia macedonica 74

lady's mantle 82
lamb's ears 63
lavender 65
Lavandula 65
Lavatera 71
Lavatera trimestris 'Mont Rose' 73
Ligularia 76
Limonium latifolium 69
Linum perenne 65

Lobelia erinus 'Cambridge Blue' 66
Lotus corniculatus 76
love-in-a-mist 68
Lychnis chalcedonica 73
Lysimachia nummularia 76
Lythrum salicaria
    'Dropmore Purple' 74
Lythrum salicaria 'Robert' 74

Macleaya cordata 80
Macleaya microcarpa
    'Kelway's Coral Plume' 80
Malva 71
Marigold 77
Meidiland roses 110
Michaelmas daisy 64
mignonette 83
Mimulus 80
moneywort 76
monkey flower 80
monkshood 66

nasturtium 76
Nepeta 65
nicotiana 83
Nicotiana langsdorfii 83
Nicotiana sanderae
    'Lime Green' 83
Nigella damascena 68

Oenothera missouriensis 77
Oenothera tetragona 77
Oenothera tetragona
    'Fyrverkeri' 77

Paeonia 'Sarah Bernhardt' 71
pansy 70
Papaver glaucum 74
Papaver nudicaule 74, 82
Papaver rhoeas 74
Papaver somniferum 70, 74
Papaver somniferum
    'Black Paeony' 70
Papaver somniferum
    'Purple Paeony' 70
Penstemon 74
peony 71
Perovskia atriplicifolia
    'Blue Spire' 65
Petunia 76
Phlox paniculata 69
Phlox paniculata hybrids 69
Phlox paniculata 'The King' 69
Phlox paniculata
    'Otley Purple' 69
Phlox paniculata 'Purple Coat 69
Phlox subulata 68
Physostegia virginiana 'Vivid' 72
Polemonium caeruleum 65
Polemonium reptans
    'Blue Pearl' 65
Polygonum amplexicaule 73
Polygonum capitatum 73
poppy 74
Potentilla 'Gibson's Scarlet' 73
Potentilla nepalensis
    'Miss Willmott' 72
Potentilla tonguei 80
Prunus spinosa 55

remantant roses 99
Reseda odorata 83
rock rose 76
Rosa 'Abraham Darby' 52, 100, 120, 121
Rosa 'Adelaïde d'Orleans' 117
Rosa 'Albéric Barbier' 14, 17
Rosa 'Albertine' 14, 68, 117
Rosa 'Alexander' 126
Rosa 'All That Jazz' 126
Rosa 'Aloha' 121
Rosa 'Alpine Sunset' 14, 126
Rosa 'Altissimo' 121
Rosa 'Amber Queen' 17, 130
Rosa 'Amsterdam' 15, 16, 17, 130
Rosa 'Anneke Doorenbos' 130
Rosa 'Aurora' 57
Rosa 'Baby Faurax' 84
Rosa 'Ballerina' 17, 54, 112
Rosa 'Bantry Bay' 13, 52, 75, 121, 123
Rosa 'Baron Girod de l'Ain' 99
Rosa 'Baroness Rothschild' 99
Rosa 'Bayernland Cover' 136
Rosa 'Belle de Crécy' 91
Rosa 'Belle Isis' 91
Rosa 'Bellevue' 126, 127
Rosa 'Betty Prior' 131
Rosa 'Bibi Maizon' 98, 100
Rosa 'Big Daddy' 127
Rosa 'Bingo Mediland' 111
Rosa 'Blanc Double de Coubert' 29, 112
Rosa 'Blanchefleur' 95
Rosa 'Blessings' 65, 127
Rosa 'Bleu Magenta' 117
Rosa 'Bleuenette' 15
Rosa 'Blossom Time' 121
Rosa 'Blush Noisette' 117
Rosa 'Bobbie James' 50, 116, 117
Rosa 'Bonica' 81, 131, 133
Rosa 'Boule de Neige' 98
Rosa 'Bourbon Queen' 98
Rosa 'Bourgogne' 23, 112
Rosa 'Brother Cadfael' 100
Rosa 'Buff Beauty' 51, 117
Rosa 'Canary Bird' 113
Rosa 'Cappa Magna' 16, 17, 113
Rosa 'Cardinal de Richelieu' 91
Rosa 'Celestial' 95
Rosa 'Celsiana' 93
Rosa 'Centenaire de Lourdes' 64, 131
Rosa 'Chapeau de Napoleon' (Rosa x centifolia 'Cristata') 40, 96
Rosa 'Charles Austin' 11, 100
Rosa 'Charles de Mills' 91
Rosa 'Charles Rennie Macintosh' 100
Rosa 'Charmian' 99, 100
Rosa 'Chicago Peace' 127
Rosa 'Chimo' 16, 54, 111
Rosa 'Chinatown' 131
Rosa 'Cinderella' 136
Rosa 'City of Belfast' 17, 131
Rosa 'City of York' 117
Rosa 'Clair Martin' 52, 121

Rosa 'Climbing Iceberg' 40, 121
Rosa 'Colibri' 17
Rosa 'Commandant Beaurepaire' 98
Rosa 'Compassion' 52, 121
Rosa 'Complicata' 95
Rosa 'Comte de Chambord' 94
Rosa 'Comtesse de Murinais' 97
Rosa 'Conditorum' 92
Rosa 'Constance Spry' 100, 117
Rosa 'Coppélia' 16, 67, 131
Rosa 'Coral Dawn' 52, 121
Rosa 'Corrie' 127
Rosa 'Cottage Rose' 101
Rosa 'The Countryman' 103
Rosa 'Coventry Cathedral' 131
Rosa 'Cupid' 117
Rosa 'Cymbeline' 101
Rosa 'Dagmar Hastrup' 113
Rosa 'Dainty Bess' 36, 127
Rosa 'Dame de Coeur' 16, 127
Rosa 'Dark Lady' 101
Rosa 'Daylight' 17, 131
Rosa 'De Meaux' 96
Rosa 'Devon' 51, 54, 58
Rosa 'Diablotin' 16, 131
Rosa 'Die Welt' 127
Rosa 'Directeur H.J. Bos' 17
Rosa 'Dorothy Perkins' 67, 118
Rosa 'Dortmund' 42, 121
Rosa 'Duchesse d'Angoulême' 92
Rosa 'Duchesse de Montebello' 92
Rosa 'Dutch Gold' 127
Rosa 'Eagle' 15, 16, 127
Rosa 'Elegant Pearl' 136
Rosa 'Elka Gaarlandt' 16
Rosa 'Elmshorn' 71
Rosa 'Emanuel' 101
Rosa 'Emily Gray' 118
Rosa 'Empress Josephine' (Rosa x francofurtana) 92
Rosa 'English Garden' 10, 101
Rosa 'Ernest H. Morse' 127
Rosa 'Escapade' 16, 131, 132
Rosa 'Esperanza' 16, 17
Rosa 'Essex' 51, 54, 58, 88
Rosa 'Evelyn' 101
Rosa 'Excelsa' 19, 45, 50
Rosa 'Eye Appeal' 111
Rosa 'Eyeopener' 58, 112
Rosa 'Eyepaint' 75
Rosa 'Fair Bianca' 100, 101
Rosa 'Fair Play' 51
Rosa 'The Fairy' 51, 54, 58, 115
Rosa 'Fantin Latour' 64, 96
Rosa 'Félicité et Perpétue' 50, 118, 120
Rosa 'Félicité Parmentier' 95
Rosa 'Ferdy' 58
Rosa 'Fervid' 17, 131
Rosa 'Finnstar' 15, 136
Rosa 'First Love' 127
Rosa 'Fisherman's Friend' 100, 101
Rosa 'Flammentanz' 120, 122
Rosa 'Fleurette' 16, 17, 54, 112
Rosa 'Fragrant Delight' 16, 131
Rosa 'Francine Austin' 101
Rosa 'Francis E. Lester' 118
Rosa 'François Juranville' 118

Rosa 'Frau Karl Druschki' 99, 122
Rosa 'Freedom' 16, 132
Rosa 'Fresh Pink' 136
Rosa 'The Friar' 42
Rosa 'Friesia' 16, 132
Rosa 'Frühlingsanfang' 113
Rosa 'Frühlingsduft' 113
Rosa 'Frühlingsmorgen' 113
Rosa 'Frühlingsschnee' 113
Rosa 'Général Kléber' 97
Rosa 'Gentle Cover' 136
Rosa 'Gertrude Jekyll' 101
Rosa 'Gisselfeldt' 16, 127
Rosa 'Glamis Castle' 102
Rosa 'Gloire de Dijon' 118
Rosa 'Gloire de France' 92
Rosa 'Golden Celebration' 102
Rosa 'Golden Showers' 122
Rosa 'Golden Wings' 113
Rosa 'Goldmarie' 17
Rosa 'Goldstern' 122
Rosa 'Golf' 83, 113
Rosa 'Graham Thomas' 76, 101, 102
Rosa 'Great Maiden's Blush' 7, 95
Rosa 'Green Snake' 113
Rosa 'Guirlande d'Amour' 15, 50, 122
Rosa 'Handel' 122
Rosa 'Hansa' 113
Rosa 'Helga' 17
Rosa 'Henri Martin' 97
Rosa 'Heritage' 102
Rosa 'Honorine de Brabant' 98
Rosa 'Iceberg' 132
Rosa 'Immensee' 113
Rosa 'Imperial Palace' 134
Rosa 'Ingrid Bergman' 14, 16, 17, 127
Rosa 'Irene of Denmark' 132
Rosa 'Ispahan' 94
Rosa 'Jan Spek' 16, 17
Rosa 'Jayne Austin' 102
Rosa 'Jeanne de Montfort' 97
Rosa 'Julischka' 17
Rosa 'Just Joey' 14, 128, 139
Rosa 'Kathleen' 114
Rosa 'Kathryn Morley' 20, 102
Rosa 'Kent' 14, 54, 58
Rosa 'Kew Rambler' 50, 89
Rosa 'Kiese' 106
Rosa 'Kirsten Poulsen' 86, 132
Rosa 'Königin von Dänemarck' 95
Rosa 'L.D. Braithwaite' 102
Rosa 'La France' 14
Rosa 'La Ville de Bruxelles' 94
Rosa 'Lady Hillingdon' 118
Rosa 'Lady of the Dawn' 16, 132
Rosa 'Landora' 128
Rosa 'Lavender Dream' 16, 54, 55, 114
Rosa 'Leander' 102, 118, 119
Rosa 'Leersum 700' 16, 132
Rosa 'Lia' 136
Rosa 'Lili Marlene' 17
Rosa 'Lilian Austin' 102
Rosa 'Little Flirt' 87, 136
Rosa 'Little White Pet' 58
Rosa 'Louise Odier' 98, 99

Rosa 'Lucetta' 102
Rosa 'Lykkefund' 119
Rosa 'Macblooba' 83
Rosa 'Magic Carousel' 136
Rosa 'Maigold' 114
Rosa 'Make-up' 16
Rosa 'Margaret Hilling' 114
Rosa 'Margaret Merril' 132
Rosa 'Maria Hofker' 128
Rosa 'Maria Mathilda' 16, 17, 132, 137
Rosa 'Mariandel' 17
Rosa 'Marie Louise' 94
Rosa 'Mary Rose' 102
Rosa 'Max Graf' 58, 114
Rosa 'Maxima' (Alba Maxima) 95
Rosa 'Memento' 16, 132
Rosa 'Mermaid' 37, 119
Rosa 'Metro' 128, 138
Rosa 'Milrose' 17
Rosa 'Minirette' 136
Rosa 'Mme Alfred Carrière' 119
Rosa 'Mme Caroline Testout' 12, 119
Rosa 'Mme Grégoire Staechelin' 118, 119, 124
Rosa 'Mme Hardy' 94
Rosa 'Mme Isaac Pereire' 98, 101
Rosa 'Mme Plantier' 38, 95
Rosa 'Monique' 20
Rosa 'Mountbatten' 17, 132
Rosa 'Mousseline' 97
Rosa 'Moyé Hammerberg' 114
Rosa 'Mozart' 36, 114
Rosa 'Mr Bluebird' 136
Rosa 'Mrs John Laing' 14, 99
Rosa 'Mullard Jubilee' 16, 128
Rosa 'Nevada' 15, 114
Rosa 'New Dawn' 50, 122
Rosa 'New Face' 51
Rosa 'New Zealand' 128
Rosa 'Nirvana' 16, 132
Rosa 'Nozomi' 19, 54, 58, 114
Rosa 'Officinalis' 92
Rosa 'Orange Fire' 16
Rosa 'Orange Sensation' 17
Rosa 'Orangeade' 132
Rosa 'Othello' 26, 103
Rosa 'Paprika' 17
Rosa 'Parade' 122
Rosa 'Parkdirektor Riggers' 122
Rosa 'Pascali' 128
Rosa 'Paso Doble' 17
Rosa 'Paul Noël' 122
Rosa 'Paul's Himalayan Musk' 50, 119
Rosa 'Paul's Lemon Pillar' 50, 119
Rosa 'Paul's Scarlet Climber' 122
Rosa 'Peace' 15, 17, 128
Rosa 'Peach Blossom' 103
Rosa 'Pearl Drift' 68
Rosa 'Pearl Meidiland' 111
Rosa 'Peaudouce' 14, 16, 52, 129
Rosa 'Peer Gynt' 129, 130
Rosa 'Penthouse' 129
Rosa 'Perdita' 103
Rosa 'Pernille Poulsen' 133
Rosa 'Persian Yellow' 114
Rosa 'Petit Four' 136

Rosa 'Petite de Hollande' 96
Rosa 'Petite Lisette' 94
Rosa 'Phyllis Bide' 119
Rosa 'Picture' 41, 129
Rosa 'The Pilgrim' 103
Rosa 'Pink Chimo' 16, 112
Rosa 'Pink Cloud' 123
Rosa 'Pink Cover' 85
Rosa 'Pink Magic' 15
Rosa 'Pink Ocean' 15, 123
Rosa 'Pink Parfait' 131, 132
Rosa 'Pink Reflection' 15, 136
Rosa 'Pink Spray' 58, 114
Rosa 'Poker' 15, 16, 129
Rosa 'Polar Star' 129
Rosa 'Polareis' 111
Rosa 'Poppy Flash' 87
Rosa 'Pretty Jessica' 102, 103
Rosa 'Prima Ballerina' 129, 130
Rosa 'The Prince' 104
Rosa 'Pristine' 129
Rosa 'Pussta' 16
Rosa 'Quatre Saisons' 94
Rosa 'Queen Elizabeth' 16, 17, 133
Rosa 'Queen of Denmark' 56
Rosa 'Rainy Day' 16
Rosa 'Rambling Rector' 120
Rosa 'Raubritter' 51
Rosa 'Red Ballerina' 115
Rosa 'Red Meidiland' 111
Rosa 'Red Star' 35, 129
Rosa 'Redouté' 103
Rosa 'Reine des Violettes' 99
Rosa 'Release' 16, 129
Rosa 'Robin Hood' 115
Rosa 'Robin Redbreast' 136
Rosa 'Rock & Roll' 17
Rosa 'Romance' 16, 17
Rosa 'Rosy Carpet' 112
Rosa 'Rosy Cushion' 17, 112
Rosa 'Rush' 15, 115
Rosa 'Saint Cecilia' 103
Rosa 'Sally Holmes' 115
Rosa 'Sander's White' 120
Rosa 'Sarabande' 16
Rosa 'Satchmo' 17
Rosa 'Scarlet Queen Elizabeth' 17
Rosa 'Scented Air' 17
Rosa 'Scharlachglut' 92
Rosa 'Seagull' 50, 120
Rosa 'Semi-Plena' 95
Rosa 'Sexy Rexy' 133
Rosa 'Sharifa Asma' 103
Rosa 'Shropshire Lass' 103
Rosa 'Silver Jubilee' 10, 129
Rosa 'Silver Rider' 15
Rosa 'Silver River' 115

Rosa 'Sir Walter Raleigh' 61, 103
Rosa 'Smarty' 112, 115
Rosa 'Souvenir de
la Malmaison' 25, 98
Rosa 'Souvenir de St Anne's' 25, 98
Rosa 'Stanwell Perpetual' 28
Rosa 'Suntan' 16, 136
Rosa 'Sun Cover' 136
Rosa 'Super Star' 17, 129
Rosa 'Swany' 51, 58
Rosa 'Sweet Juliet' 103
Rosa 'Sweetheart' 19, 130
Rosa 'Sylphide' 15, 133
Rosa 'Sympathie' 52, 123
Rosa 'Tapis Volant' 15, 51, 58, 115
Rosa 'Thalia' 120
Rosa 'Tojo' 16
Rosa 'Tour de Malakoff' 96
Rosa 'Tricolore de Flandre' 92
Rosa 'Trier 2000' 16, 17
Rosa 'Troika' 16, 130
Rosa 'True Love' 130
Rosa 'Tuscany' 93
Rosa 'Tuscany Superb' 93
Rosa 'Twinkle' 136
Rosa 'Variegata di Bologna' 99
Rosa 'Veilchenblau' 120
Rosa 'Versicolor' 93
Rosa 'Warwick Castle' 24, 104
Rosa 'Wedding Day' 50, 82, 120,
122
Rosa 'Weisse Immensee' 115
Rosa 'Wendy Cussons' 17, 130
Rosa 'White Dorothy Perkins' 120
Rosa 'White Fleurette' 16, 54, 112
Rosa 'White Spray' 58, 115
Rosa 'White Wings' 46, 130
Rosa 'Wife of Bath' 104
Rosa 'William Lobb' 97
Rosa 'William Shakespeare' 61,
104
Rosa 'Winchester Cathedral' 104
Rosa 'Windrush' 104
Rosa 'Yellow Button' 76, 104
Rosa 'Yellow Fleurette' 16, 112
Rosa 'The Yeoman' 32, 104
Rosa 'Zéphirine Drouhin'
Rosa 'Zwergkönig' 136
Rosa x alba 94
Rosa arvensis 58, 106
Rosa banksiae 106
Rosa banksiae 'Lutea' 106
Rosa canina 9, 56, 105, 106
Rosa centifolia 27, 95
Rosa x centifolia 'Cristata' 40
Rosa x damascena 93
Rosa filipes 50, 107, 108

Rosa filipes 'Kiftsgate' 50, 107, 118
Rosa gallica 91
Rosa gallica 'Conditorum' 11
Rosa gallica 'Officinalis' 91
Rosa gallica 'Versicolor' 93
Rosa glauca 56, 105, 107
Rosa glauca 'Carminetta' 39, 107
Rosa gymnocarpa 69
Rosa hibernica (x) 26, 107
Rosa hugonis 107
Rosa longicuspis 47, 50
Rosa majalis 71, 107
Rosa x mariae-graebnerae 56,
108
Rosa mollis 22, 108
Rosa moschata 34, 92, 96
Rosa moyesii 56, 115
Rosa moyesii 'Geranium' 56, 108
Rosa moyesii 'Ina Belder' 56, 108
Rosa multiflora 50, 105, 108, 109
Rosa nitida 56, 77, 105, 108
Rosa omeiensis f. pteracantha 108
Rosa paulii 58
Rosa pimpinellifolia 9, 56, 109
Rosa pimpinellifolia
'Glory of Edsel' 9
Rosa pimpinellifolia 'Mary
Queen of Scott's' 9
Rosa rubiginosa 9, 56, 105, 109,
111
Rosa rugosa 55, 105, 109
Rosa rugosa 'Agnes' 109
Rosa rugosa 'Max Graf' 109
Rosa rugosa 'Red Max Graf' 58
Rosa rugosa 'Roseraie de l'Hay'
110
Rosa rugosa 'Sarah Van Fleet' 110
Rosa rugosa 'Schneezwerg' 110
Rosa rugosa 'White Captain' 32,
69, 110
Rosa rugosa 'White Max Graf' 58
Rosa setipoda 82, 110
Rosa villosa 110
Rosa virginiana 55, 105, 110
Rosa virginiana 'Harvest Song' 55
Rudbeckia 76

sage 68
Salvia coccinea 75
Salvia farinacea 'Blue Bedder' 68
Salvia horminum 68
Salvia nemerosa 'Blauhügel' 68
Salvia nemerosa 'Elisabeth' 68
Salvia nemerosa 'Mainacht' 68
Salvia nemerosa 'Ostfriesland' 67
Salvia officinalis 68
Salvia patens 68

Salvia sclarea 72
Scabiosa atropurpurea 75
Scabiosa caucasica 65
Scabiosa ochroleuca 75
Scotch rose 9
sea lavender, statice 69
Senecio bicolor 65
Sidalcea 'Elsie Heugh' 71
Solidago 77
Solidaster luteus 77
snapdragon 77
speedwell 64
standard roses:
apricot 138
yellow 138
orange 139
red 139
pink 139
white 138
sunflower 77

Taxus baccata 55
Telekia 76
Teucrium x lucidrys 44
Thalictrum aquifolium
'Thundercloud' 69
Thalictrum delavayi
'Hewitt's Double' 69
Thalictrum rochebrunianum
69
thistle 64
Tithonia rotundifolia 81
Tropaeolum majus 'Primrose
Jewel' 76

Verbena bipinnatifida 70
Verbena bonariensis 70
Verbena canadensis 70
Verbena hybrids 75
Verbena rigida 70
Veronica filiformis 64
Veronica longifolia 68
Veronica spicata subsp. incana
(syn. Veronica incana) 68
Veronica waldsteinii 68
Viola 'Baby Franjo' 82
Viola cornuta 'Admiration' 70
Viola cornuta
'Primrose Dame' 75
Viola cornuta 'Roem
van Aalsmeer' 70
Viola cornuta 'W.H. Woodgate' 70

yarrow 80
yew 55

Zinnia 82

Acknowledgement
The publisher and author would like to thank
Wim Snoeyer of Gouda for his invaluable
help in the realization of this book.